Engage Striving
Students IN THE
Common Core Classroom

JANE FEBER

Engage Striving Students in the Common Core Classroom

by Jane Feber

© 2014 Jane Feber

Cover Illustration: Sandra D'Antonio
Composition/design: Studio Montage

Library of Congress Cataloging-in-Publication Data
>
Feber, Jane, 1951-
Strategies to engage struggling and not-so-struggling students in the
common core classroom / Jane Feber.
pages cm
Includes bibliographical references.
ISBN 978-1-62521-510-9 (pbk.)
1. Reading—Remedial teaching—United States. 2. Language
arts—Curricula—United States. 3. Language arts—Standards—United
States. 4. Creative activities and seat work—United States. I. Title.

LB1050.5.F36 2013
372.43—dc23
>
2013024742

Maupin House publishes professional development resources for K-12 educators.
Contact us for tailored, in-school training or to schedule an author for a workshop or conference.
Visit www.maupinhouse.com for free lesson plan downloads.

Maupin House Publishing, Inc. by Capstone Professional

1710 Roe Crest Drive
North Mankato, MN 56003
www.maupinhouse.com
800-524-0634
352-373-5546 (fax)
info.maupinhouse.com

10 9 8 7 6 5 4 3 2 1

Photo Credits
Shutterstock: Matin, 12, Sari ONeal, 12, kyynzq, 12, topseller, 12

Printed in the United States of America in Eau Claire, Wisconsin.
092013   07786

Dedication

Thanks to all of the students who showed me that the activities in this book are truly engaging and to the teachers who allowed me the privilege of working with their students. And to my BFF, Diane Bondurant, who is always willing to be my sounding board.

"Success is not measured by heights obtained...but by obstacles overcome."

—Author unknown

TABLE OF CONTENTS

ADDITIONAL RESOURCES

INTRODUCTION

Why I Wrote This Book

Many students struggle in school. They often move from grade to grade, falling further and further behind. By the time they reach middle school, these children are experienced struggling students. They are turned off to learning; it's our job to turn them back on. To do this, we must actively engage them in the learning process. Not only must students learn to comprehend text, they must also learn to make connections and think critically when reading. "True comprehension goes beyond literal understanding and involves the reader's interaction with text. If students are to become thoughtful, insightful readers, they must merge their thinking with the text and extend their thinking beyond a superficial understanding" (Harvey and Goudvis 2007).

In the state of Florida, middle and high school teachers who work with struggling readers are required to take 300 hours of reading instruction in order to add a reading endorsement to their teaching certificate. For the past seven years, I have been teaching the last class of this reading endorsement, Reading Competency 5 (formerly Reading Competency 6). This class consists of twelve hours of facilitation detailing how to put together a portfolio that includes case studies on three students, with instructional practices to assist students with the five strands of reading— phonemic awareness, phonics, fluency, vocabulary, and comprehension— plus five lesson plans, which are then recorded as teachers incorporate the gradual release model (Gallagher and Pearson 1983). Teachers must teach one lesson for each of these strands of reading.

PHONEMIC AWARENESS AND PHONICS

These middle and high school teachers are often very uncomfortable with the idea of teaching lessons in phonemic awareness and phonics, thinking their students will find it babyish. "We don't teach phonemic awareness and phonics (and often fluency) in middle school and high school!" they cry. I assure them as they review their recorded lessons and write their reflections, they will see how necessary it is to teach phonemic awareness and phonics to struggling readers. And they do. These students need tools to assist them with decoding unfamiliar words. Yet we can't teach phonemic awareness and phonics to middle and high school students in the same way we teach elementary students. That said, teachers of the elementary grades will find the activities provided in this book applicable in their classrooms, as do the elementary education teachers who chose to enroll in my Reading Competency class.

TEXT COMPLEXITY

In the twenty-first century, all teachers are now teachers of reading. Whether you formally teach reading, language arts, science or social studies, your students are reading. And with the Common Core State Standards (CCSS) in place, text complexity is the order of the day. With text complexity comes the need for text-dependent questions to ensure that students are making sense of the written word. Answering text-dependent questions requires students to answer questions based specifically on content. With previous standards, students might have been asked "why" questions or had to answer questions where they went outside the text and made personal connections. Well-designed text-dependent questions require students to analyze the text carefully and to read word by word, phrase by phrase, and sentence by sentence—thus the need for students to be able to decode words, read fluently, and establish a strong vocabulary. In order to meet the Common Core State Standards, students must be able to analyze, probe, and examine the text in order to extract meaning.

VOCABULARY: ENCOURAGING PERSONAL CONNECTIONS AND METACOGNITION

Vocabulary is the meat and potatoes of comprehension. Without a substantial vocabulary, comprehension is meaningless. Students must develop complete concept knowledge of words they encounter. They must develop strategies to be able to make connections to words and be provided a variety of activities to use new words. According to Robert Marzano (2004), students need multiple exposures to a word before they understand it while reading and can use it in their own speaking and writing. All students require vocabulary development, especially English language learners, students from low socioeconomic areas, and students who are struggling readers.

Words! Words! Words! Words are our oral and written form of expression. Therefore, the larger our vocabulary, the more effectively we can communicate in both oral and written form. In order to become proficient in any academic area, students must develop a wide breadth of academic vocabulary. Janet Allen (2007) tells us, "The why of vocabulary instruction is easily answered: in the absence of a repertoire of effective instructional strategies for teaching those words that are critical to students understandings of a variety of texts, they will continue to struggle in their content classes."

The Common Core State Standards place an emphasis on vocabulary development, not only in language arts and reading, but also in the content areas. Students must be able to decipher unfamiliar vocabulary as well as phrases, which will lead to ultimate understanding of the text.

As I learned from teaching my students, making personal connections to vocabulary words is an effective way to teach vocabulary. These connections encourage students to think about the words they must learn. The vocabulary activities in this book allow for just that. "Background knowledge of vocabulary and concepts are an integral part of comprehension. It is extremely difficult for young readers to construct knowledge from something they are reading if the topic and important vocabulary are completely foreign" (Kelley and Clausen-Grace 2007).

Metacognition allows students to think about what they are thinking. By making connections, asking questions, and visualizing what they are reading, students become more proficient readers. Vocabulary is key because without words we have no sentences, no paragraphs, and ultimately no text.

VOCABULARY: PROVIDING INSTRUCTIONAL VARIETY
As Carol Jago (2011) states in her book, *With Rigor for All: Meeting Common Core Standards for Reading Literature*, "Students need a robust vocabulary not only to read literature but also to express what they think about what they are reading." Since students learn new vocabulary in a variety of different ways, we must provide a toolkit of many strategies to learn new words. The traditional vocabulary instruction whereby students look up words in the dictionary is no longer effective. Often definitions are not clear to the students because they don't understand the words used in the definition. The vocabulary activities in this book have been tried with students in many classroom situations. Students actually get excited about learning new words when the activities are engaging. And the learning sticks!

STUDENT ENGAGEMENT
As with everything done in the classroom, student engagement is the key to learning. "The amount of student learning and personal development associated with any educational program is directly proportional to the quality and quantity of student involvement in that program" (National

Institute of Education 1984). Research shows that engaged students learn more, retain more, and enjoy learning more than students who are not engaged (Dowson and McInerney 2001; Hancock and Betts 2002; Lumsden 1994; Voke 2002). In my book *Student Engagement Is FUNdamental* (2011), I provide a variety of activities that allow teachers to get to know their students. Today's students come to school with much baggage, and it's the teacher's job to know the students. Once a positive rapport is established in the classroom, students feel comfortable making mistakes and can learn from their mistakes. Students also learn to respect their fellow classmates and the fact that individual differences are what make the world go round.

The activities presented in this book engage students as they are required to become metacognitive about words. Opportunities are presented for students to ask questions, visualize, and become creative when working with new words. According to Camille Blachowicz and Peter Fisher (2002), the effective vocabulary teacher presents new vocabulary in ways that model good learning. This type of instruction develops learners who are active, who personalize their learning, who look for multiple sources of information to build meaning, and who are playful with words. Good learners are active. As in all learning situations, having the learners actively attempting to construct their own meanings is a hallmark of good instruction.

Students are accustomed to multi-tasking and staying busy. Educators must use this to engage today's students. Ask your students if they prefer engagement or boredom. A study conducted by the Bill and Melinda Gates Foundation (2006), "The Silent Epidemic: Perspectives of High School Dropouts," found that nearly 50 percent of 470 dropouts surveyed said they left school because their classes were boring. This is quite an indication that students would rather be engaged than bored. Students who are engaged learn at higher levels, have a more profound grasp of what they learn, retain what they learn, and can transfer what they learn to new contexts (The Schelchty Center for Leadership in School Reform 2009).

How This Book Is Organized

It is my goal for the activities in this book to provide intervention for adolescent students who are struggling with the reading process. With the Common Core State Standards in place in more states than not, I want teachers to be able to align the activities in this book with those standards.

I also chose to align the activities with the College and Career Readiness Anchor Standards, assuming that teachers at various grade levels will be able to adapt the activities with increasing rigor at each grade level.

Where activities in the book might call for the reading of one text at a certain grade level, teachers of upper grades can instruct students to compare two or more texts. The College and Career Readiness Anchor Standards and the grade-specific standards are necessary complements—the former providing broad standards, the latter providing additional specificity—that together define the skills and understandings that all students must demonstrate (CCSS 2010, 35).

Since the activities presented in this book focus on interventions for struggling readers, I chose to address standards for Reading: Literature and Informational Text (to assist with reading comprehension and analysis), Speaking and Listening (to assist with fluency), and Reading: Foundational Skills (to provide instructional practices in decoding). Although the foundational skills are standards addressed in kindergarten through fifth grade, older students who are struggling might not have become proficient in this area. Since there are no anchor standards for the foundational skills, I chose the ones for grades four and five, as these standards address the decoding activities presented in this book that will assist struggling adolescent readers with their reading deficiency.

The book is organized alphabetically by activity name with a notation after each activity explaining whether it focuses on Literature, Informational Text, Speaking and Listening, or Foundational Skills. Several activities cover more than one area, such as literature and informational text. As you will notice, the writing and language standards are not addressed in this book since the focus of this book is on instructional practices to engage students in becoming proficient in the five strands of reading: phonemic awareness (Foundational Skills), phonics (Foundational Skills), fluency (Speaking and Listening), and vocabulary and comprehension (Reading: Literature and Informational Text).

As teachers are the ones who know their students best, activities can be pulled from each category to assist students in areas of weakness. Once students become cognizant of the fact that they must be able to decode words, read fluently, and build their vocabulary, comprehension will follow.

Comprehension Rationale

Think of how frustrating it is when you are driving down the road and your car quits and you do not know the cause or—worse—how to fix it… or when you wake up in the morning and walk into the bathroom to a soggy floor because the toilet seal is leaking and you don't know what to do…or when tax time arrives and you do not understand how to fill in all the blanks. This is how our struggling students feel all the time as they occupy the seats in our classrooms. Whenever I travel to a non-English-speaking country, I pick up local newspapers and find myself feeling as our students must when they pick up textbooks. I look at the foreign words in the newspapers and feel lost.

Today's classrooms are melting pots of readers ranging from the avid reader who always has a book nearby, reads every book in a series and thirsts for more, to the struggling reader who calls out words with so little fluency that there is no meaning attached to what has been read.

So how do we recognize struggling students who are unable to comprehend text? The following is an abbreviated list of characteristics taken from *When Kids Can't Read: What Teachers Can Do* (Beers 2003):
- Does not set a purpose for reading other than to complete the assignment
- Does not connect events in the text to other texts or to events in personal experience
- Does not recognize cause and effect relationships
- Does not read to clarify meaning
- Does not visualize the text

So, what do we, as teachers, do to assist struggling readers in comprehending text? We must first make sure they understand what reading strategies are and how to use them. Laura Robb (1996) says that a skill becomes a strategy when the learner can use it independently, when she can reflect on and understand how it works and then apply it to new reading material. Becoming a proficient reader does not occur overnight; one must take baby steps before one can walk. Chris Tovani (2000) states that readers need to construct their own meaning. In order to do this, they need to apply reading strategies—conscientiously at first, but eventually it becomes more automatic. By learning to apply reading strategies, students learn to become active readers as opposed to passive readers. Long gone are the days of rote memorization and worksheets; long gone are silent classrooms with students sitting quietly in rows; long gone is the teacher lecturing. Today's students are used to multitasking and need to be engaged in the learning process.

The times and our students are changing. Technology, texting, tweeting, blogging, and Facebooking are new ways to communicate. It seems as though many students spend more time playing video games than reading books. As the times change, so must our teaching strategies. Engagement is key. Research shows that engaged students learn more, retain more, and enjoy learning more than students who are not engaged (Dowson and McInerney 2001; Hancock and Betts 2002; Lumsden 1994; Voke 2002). Active engagement can lead students to make knowledge their own. Mere regurgitation of facts and figures, without a deep rooting in the reasoning behind such information, is not sufficient for in-depth understanding. Active engagement in learning affords students a greater range of understanding (National Center for Research on Teacher Learning 1993).

Before students can become actively engaged, they must understand what is expected of them. This is where teacher modeling becomes imperative. Yet teacher modeling alone is no longer the answer. The gradual release of responsibility model (Pearson and Gallagher 1983) shifts the cognitive load from teacher modeling of "I do" to the collaboration of "We do" to the application level and independence of "You do." By implementing this gradual release model, teachers assist students in establishing confidence. Students gradually learn to apply reading strategies that allow them to comprehend text at higher cognitive levels of analysis, synthesis, and evaluation and to become involved in their learning.

Over the years, as I ask students why they don't ask questions, their response is always the same. "When you ask questions, everyone thinks you are dumb." In order to become a proficient reader, students must understand that asking questions is the smart thing to do. Asking questions is a key reading strategy to assist in clarifying information presented in the text. Proficient readers also understand that they learn from their mistakes, and they understand that reading and thinking go hand in hand. Comprehension requires thinking, and students who do not comprehend text must be taught how to think—how to process information set before them in print. Since not all text is easy to understand, students must recognize that chunking the text and re-reading are strategies often employed by even the best readers. And, most importantly, proficient readers think about what they are thinking as they read; they are metacognitive.

The comprehension activities presented in this book encourage students to think about what they are reading and to analyze, synthesize, and evaluate. Once students begin to process information and make it personal, learning will take place.

Speaking & Listening Rationale

Developing fluent readers is an often neglected practice in the upper grades. Yet the bridge between decoding and comprehension is reading fluency (Rasinski 2004). It's imperative for struggling readers to hear modeling of fluent reading, repeat their reading, learn how to stop or pause when punctuation is present, and most importantly, comprehend the text. "Fluency is not merely lining up one sentence after another and reading them aloud quickly; it's also maintaining understanding across a text" (Shanahan, Fisher, and Frey 2012, 61). Fluency is a two-fold process that requires decoding and comprehending text at the same time. Readers often struggle due to the fact that they are unable to decode vocabulary within the text.

In order to be considered fluent readers, students must read in a way that sounds natural. Hesitating, struggling to decode words, and reading aloud without expression hinder the fluent reading process. Disfluent readers often read word by word, so by the time they reach the end of a sentence, all meaning is lost. According to Richard Allington (2009), in order to become fluent readers, it is necessary for students to develop the following:

- Appropriate decoding skills and strategies
- A large vocabulary of words whose meaning they know
- A store of words they can recognize at a glance
- The ability to self-monitor while they read
- The appropriate comprehension strategies to use while they read (see page 18 for the "Reading Strategies" mini-book)
- The motivation to read purposely and voluntarily

With the Common Core State Standards, speaking and listening are now receiving more attention, and reader's theater can provide a vehicle for students to practice both skills. Once the teacher has modeled fluent reading, reader's theater offers an engaging way for students to practice repeated readings. Richard Allington (2009) states, "It now seems clear that the major reason for the success of repeated readings as an intervention strategy is that it expands reading volume when implemented. In other words, time spent in repeatedly reading texts replaces time that was previously spent on other activities such as skills worksheets." Reader's theater scripts are ubiquitous; you can find them on the Internet or in most literature textbooks. In order to present the script successfully to the class, students must practice repeated readings. As Timothy Rasinski (2003) explains, "Reader's theater is an authentic, entertaining, and educationally powerful way to read and communicate meaning."

Rasinski (2003) also suggests ways to build reading fluency:

- Model good oral reading. This helps students see that meaning does not only come from the words in the text but also from the expression used when reading.
- Provide oral support for readers. This can be done through paired reading, choral reading, and allowing students to listen to recorded materials.
- Offer plenty of practice opportunities. Practice makes perfect, and the more chances a student has to read a particular text, the more fluent the reader becomes.
- Encourage fluency through phrasing.

Disfluent readers must be encouraged to read frequently. I am often in middle and high school classes with struggling readers, and I watch these students pick up a book from the classroom library to read during their sustained silent reading time. During the fifteen to twenty minutes of silent reading, very few students read. When asked to get their books out the following class period, many students randomly grab a book from the class library which is not necessarily the book chosen the previous class period. So I ask these students what it would take to get them to read, and they tell me they want to read interesting books. Teachers need to get to know their students and help them locate books of interest to them. For this reason—and with the assistance of the students I work with—I developed a reading interest survey on page 127 to help teachers gather data on students' interests in order to recommend books they will enjoy. Students cannot become fluent readers if they do not read, and they will not read unless they are reading what interests them. According to Allington (1983), reading fluency plays a key role in developing effective and efficient readers. Rasinski (2004) sums up the need for fluency instruction when he states, "If fluency is a concern among middle and high school students, it needs to be taught."

Foundational Skills Rationale

One of the biggest challenges facing struggling readers is the inability to decode unfamiliar words. In early grades, students are taught letter-sound relationships. Linnea Ehri's stages of reading development (1998) indicate that pre-K and kindergarten children should be introduced to letter-sound relationships. At ages five and six, children should be able to read simple words and have a grasp of letter-sound relationships. By ages six through eight, students should be able to use their letter-sound knowledge to decode unfamiliar words, and from age seven and up, students need to be exposed to more advanced word-analysis skills. With struggling readers, it's quite evident that they did not master these skills.

A problem seen with many struggling students in middle and high school is failure to master the K-5 CCSS Foundational Skills. "The Standards set grade-specific standards but do not define the intervention methods or materials necessary to support students who are well below or well above grade-level expectations" (CCSS 2010, 6). There are no formal standards to address the development of foundational skills in the upper grades. Often intervention is necessary to provide struggling students a vehicle for decoding unfamiliar words. That's where the decoding activities in this book come into play. The activities presented are not meant to teach phonemic awareness and phonics through explicit instruction but rather to provide struggling students a way to compensate for their deficiencies by becoming reacquainted with the standards not mastered in lower levels.

Phonics is the foundation of all basic reading skills. Upper-grade students need phonics instruction. When students lack the skills necessary to decode words, they need to be taught strategies to assist them. Lack of understanding of the letter-sound relationship is one reason that many struggling readers are unable to decode words. When students learn the relationship between letter combinations and sounds, they have a tool to use when decoding unfamiliar words.

Phonics is not just for little kids. Regardless of age, if students cannot decode the graphemes (letters) and give them the appropriate sounds (phonemes), then meaning will be lost. Being able to decode words allows students to make meaning of words, phrases, sentences, and entire paragraphs. Becoming familiar with letter patterns will assist many struggling students in attaining comprehension.

According to the National Institute of Child Health and Human Development (2000), phonics instruction in early grades helps to develop a solid foundation for more advanced decoding skills. Yet when students do not master the rudiments of phonics in the early grades, the reading process becomes a downward spiral. The need to provide decoding strategies in the upper grades is clear.

However, upper-grade students are often insulted if given elementary decoding activities. To assist struggling readers in the upper grades with decoding skills, we need to make the activities engaging, challenging, and age appropriate. We also need to take them back to the elementary strategies they might not have mastered: recognizing beginning, middle, and ending sounds; chunking word parts to assist with decoding; learning syllable patterns; and recognizing that, as letters in a word are rearranged, their sounds might change.

As stated in *The Struggling Reader: Interventions That Work*, "If the student is like most struggling readers, he or she has been taught the skill in the past but did not learn it" (Cooper, Chard, and Kiger 2006, 65). It is our job as teachers to make sure that our struggling readers master decoding skills and recognize that decoding is the key that unlocks the door to reading proficiency.

ACTIVITIES

Anticipation Box/Collage

COMMON CORE
STATE STANDARDS
Literature 1, 2, 3;
Informational Text 1

Objective

To provide a vehicle for students to predict what a selection will be about; to determine how objects/ideas in a selection provide symbolism that can be analyzed once the story is completed

What the Research Says

"A well-designed anticipation guide activates and assesses students' prior knowledge, sets a purpose for reading, and helps motivate reluctant readers by stimulating their interest in the topic" (Urquhart and Frazce 2012, 15).

"Preparing students to read a text is perfectly reasonable, and it's compatible with the Common Core State Standards. But such preparation should be brief and should focus on providing students with the tools they need to make sense of the text on their own" (Shanahan 2012/2013, 11-16).

Materials

A box of artifacts symbolic to a selection

Directions

1. Before reading a selection in class, put together a box of items that symbolize events/ideas in a selection.

    a. *Holes* by Louis Sachar

        i. A shovel

        ii. A big sneaker

        iii. A yellow lizard

        iv. A lipstick

        v. A jar of peach preserves

        vi. A brochure for Camp Greenlake

    b. *The Hunger Games* by Suzanne Collins

        i. A bow and arrow

        ii. An apple

        iii. A bird

        iv. Berries

2. Instruct students to predict what each item might symbolize in the selection. Students will write the prediction in a notebook that they will be able to refer to once they complete the selection.

3. Once students have completed reading the selection, have them revisit their predictions. Then ask them to select one of the symbols discussed in the anticipation box. Instruct students to provide three reasons why this item was symbolic in the text using text-based support.

The Hunger Games **example from** *Student Engagement is FUNdamental* **by Jane Feber (2011):**

Symbol: bow and arrow

The bow and arrow represent life. Katniss used the bow and arrow to provide her family and district with food. She also traded her catch for other provisions her family needed. The bow and arrow also represent the cycle of life. Katniss was not only able to provide food for survival but also take life when she or others close to her were threatened. And initially, the bow and arrow represent protection. Katniss was not a killer. She only used the bow and arrow when her life was in danger.

Variation

Rather than an anticipation box, create an anticipation collage (*see Figure 1*) to share using the document camera or interactive Whiteboard, and follow steps 2 and 3 above.

FIGURE 1

Before/During/After Reading Mini-book

COMMON CORE
STATE STANDARDS
Literature 1, 2, 3, 6;
Informational Text 1, 2, 3, 6

Objective
To provide choice and differentiate instruction

What the Research Says
"Offering choices is one of the simplest ways to encourage student involvement in your classroom" (Blackburn 2008).

Materials
"Before, During, and After Reading Strategies" mini-book (page 18)

Directions

1. Distribute the "Before, During, and After Reading Strategies" mini-book (page 18) to students and instruct them on how to fold the paper to create a mini-book.

2. Assign a reading selection. This can be one selection read by the entire class, small groups of students reading the same selection, or each student reading something different.

3. Allow students to each select one before-reading activity from the mini-book to complete before reading the selection. Provide time for students to share their findings by grouping students according to the activity completed.

4. Once students are ready to begin reading the selection, instruct them to select one during-reading activity. Once students have completed their during-reading activity, group students who have completed the same assignment so they can share and compare notes.

5. After reading the selection, allow students to select one activity to complete. A grading rubric should be created and provided for each activity so that students know the expectations. Grading rubrics for the milk carton project and the commemorative stamps project can be found on pages 15 and 17. Additional grading rubrics can be found in *Creative Book Reports: Rubrics for Fiction and Nonfiction* by Jane Feber (2004).

Milk Carton Mobile for After-Reading Activity

NAME _____

Your task is to create a milk carton display with information on a given topic of nonfiction study. Each side of the carton will display a written description of a major component of your studies, along with an illustration.

Materials
- Clean, four-sided milk carton, painted if possible
- Wrapping paper, wallpaper, or contact paper
- Paper to draw on or illustrations from old magazines and newspapers
- Glue
- Hole punch
- Yarn or string

Directions
1. Bring a clean, four-sided milk carton from home. Paint it at home if possible.

2. Decorate your carton using wrapping paper, wallpaper, or contact paper.

3. Write the title of your project on a strip of construction paper and glue it to the top of the carton. Write your name on the bottom of the carton.

4. Plan out the space on each side of the carton so you will have room for a label, a description, and an illustration.

5. Create labels for each side of the carton and glue them on.

6. Write a description of each of the four topics and glue these on.

7. Create illustrations for each description and glue them on.

8. Punch a hole in the pouring spout of the carton and thread string or yarn through it. Cartons can now be hung for display.

excerpted from *Creative Book Reports: Fun Projects with Rubrics for Fiction and Nonfiction* by Jane Feber, Maupin House, 2004

Rubric for Nonfiction Milk Carton Mobile

_____ Carton is painted or covered attractively   **(5 points)**

_____ Project title is on the top of the carton; your name is on the bottom   **(5 points)**

_____ Each section of the carton contains a title and a well-written description or thorough research; panel is illustrated. See below for point values.

_____ Panel 1   **(15 points) Place your criteria here**

_____ Panel 2   **(15 points) Place your criteria here**

_____ Panel 3   **(15 points) Place your criteria here**

_____ Panel 4   **(15 points) Place your criteria here**

_____ Correct use of grammar, spelling, punctuation, capitalization, complete sentences   **(20 points)**

_____ Neat/attractive presentation   **(10 points)**

_____ **FINAL GRADE/100**

Stamps/Coins for After-Reading Activity

NAME _____

Your task is to create a set of three commemorative stamps or coins describing concepts, people, or events in a unit of study. You will decide whether you will prepare stamps or coins.

Materials

- Three pieces of construction paper, 5" square (stamps) or three pieces of construction paper, 5" round (coins)
- Colored pencils or markers for drawing
- Poster or tag board

Directions

1. Research concepts, people, or events in your unit of study. Pick three for your stamps or coins.

2. For stamps, you need three pieces of construction paper approximately 5" square. For coins, you need three pieces of construction paper approximately 5" round.

3. Label the stamp or coin with the title of your topic. Then write one description and provide a colorful illustration on each stamp or coin.

4. Mount them on a piece of poster board or tag board and add a title.

5. Be sure to write your name on the reverse side of the poster.

from *Creative Book Reports: Fun Projects with Rubrics for Fiction and Nonfiction* by Jane Feber, Maupin House, 2004

Rubric for Stamps/Coins

_____ Poster is titled with the topic: "Commemorative Stamps" or "Commemorative Coins" **(5 points)**

_____ Stamp or coin one is labeled and a well-developed description is provided; stamp or coin is illustrated **(20 points)**

_____ Stamp or coin two is labeled and a well-developed description is provided; stamp or coin is illustrated **(20 points)**

_____ Stamp or coin three is labeled and a well-developed description is provided; stamp or coin is illustrated **(20 points)**

_____ Correct use of grammar, spelling, punctuation, capitalization, complete sentences **(20 points)**

_____ Neat/attractive appearance **(10 points)**

_____ Your name is on the reverse side of the poster **(5 points)**

_____ **FINAL GRADE/100**

Before, During, And After Reading Strategies

Before Reading

- What is the purpose for reading this selection?
- What do the illustrations tell you about this story?
- What does the title tell you about this selection?
- If there are bold print headings, what do these tell you about this selection?

- Concept maps
- Activating prior knowledge
- K-D-L (what I know, what I don't know, what I learned)
- Anticipation guides
- A hook: movie clip, YouTube video, related children's book
- A to Z with words related to the topic of study
- Anticipation box: Place artifacts in a box; pull out one at a time while students predict what will happen in the story.

During Reading

- Learning Log
- Make predictions
- Questions I have
- Vocabulary I don't know
- Illustrations
- Notes to the characters (dialogue journal)
- **Sticky Notes**
- Interesting facts
- What's not clear

- Create a story board of important ideas.
- **Double entry journal: Place a phrase or sentence in the left column; in the right column tell what the phrase or sentence means to you.**
- **Reciprocal teaching**
  - Predicting
  - Clarifying
  - Questioning
  - Summarizing
  - Think-pair-share

After Reading

- QAR's (Question-Answer-Relationships)
- Herringbone graphic organizer
- Add to the A to Z chart
- Retelling to a partner
- One sentence summary
- **Letter to the author telling what you liked or did not like about the selection/story**
- Plot poems
- Nonfiction: Create a commemorative stamp for each person in the selection
- Create a milk carton showing one literary element on each side with an illustration

- Questions for each category of Bloom's taxonomy in the form of a flip book. **Students write and answer their questions or trade questions with another student.**
  - Remembering
  - Understanding
  - Applying
  - Analyzing
  - Evaluating
  - Creating
- Assign selections of the story to small groups and have students act out scenes.
- Create a business card for a character.

Cell Phone/Internet Vocabulary

COMMON CORE
STATE STANDARDS
Literature 4,
Informational Text 4

Objective
To provide students with a twenty-first-century way to look up vocabulary words and get a simple definition

What the Research Says
"The Internet has entered our classrooms faster than books, television, computers, the telephone, or any other technology for information and communication. Moreover, the Internet will be the vehicle for a host of new technologies that will continue to enter the classroom, regularly requiring new literacies from all of us. One of the more consistent findings from research in this area is that students are highly motivated and interested in these new literacies" (Leu 2002, 81).

Materials
Cell phone with text messaging capability (Internet is not needed) or computer with Internet access

Directions
1. Tell students they will be using technology to look up a vocabulary word. First model the activity, either using your cell phone or one belonging to a student and send an online query using one of the following methods.
   a. iPhone. Use *Siri* to send a verbal query requesting a definition: "*Siri*, what does 'ubiquitous' mean?" or download a free dictionary from the App Store.
   b. Android phone. Use the phone's browser to access Google or download a free dictionary from the Play Store.

2. Show students how to access the following online dictionaries from an Internet-connected computer, a cell phone, or an iPad/tablet.
   a. http://www.thefreedictionary.com
   b. http://www.onelook.com (this site searches a variety of dictionaries that include the word)
   c. http://www.dictionary.com (this site also answers relevant questions about the word being looked up)

3. After modeling the options above, instruct students to take out their cell phones, if they have one, or to use a classroom computer and look up a word. Students can partner up if there aren't enough devices to work individually.

4. Remind students using Google to type the word *Define* followed by a space followed by the word they want defined: *Define* ubiquitous.

5. Invite students to share with the class the various methods they used to look up words.

Cloze Paragraph

Objective
To complete a cloze-type passage sharing information about oneself

What the Research Says
"When students are asked to perform for others, they have a natural inclination and desire to practice the passage to the point where they can read it accurately, with appropriate rate, and especially with meaningful expression and phrasing" (Rasinski et al. 2005, 22-27).

Materials
"Cloze" activity sheet (page 21)

Directions
1. Tell students they are completing a cloze activity in which they will be sharing information about themselves.

2. Provide students with the "Cloze" activity sheet.

3. Model the cloze activity by sharing with the class a cloze paragraph you composed about yourself.

4. Provide time for students to complete the "Cloze" activity sheet.

5. As students finish, pair them up and have partners read their cloze paragraph to each other.

6. Once the pair has completed their reading, have the students find others who have completed their cloze paragraph and partner up with them.

7. Once all students have shared their cloze paragraph with at least two or three partners, ask the class to suggest students with interesting cloze paragraphs to share with the class. You can also put all students' names in a basket and randomly pull names of students who can share with the class.

Variation
I was doing this activity in one class and a student asked if she could fill the passage out as Batman. This led to a fun-filled activity! Students completed the cloze paragraph taking on the persona of someone else: a boyfriend, a famous athlete, and a music artist. The following day, we completed the cloze paragraph taking on the persona of characters in *The Crucible*. This activity was a hit in the classroom!

Cloze Activity Sheet

Hi, my name is _____ .

Something you should know about me is _____

_____

_____ .

When I _____,

_____

others _____

_____ .

One thing I am good at is _____

_____ .

I enjoy doing this because _____

_____ .

Yet I really am not comfortable _____

_____

because _____

_____ .

One of my goals in life is to _____

_____ .

I hope to accomplish this by _____

_____ .

Creating Words Card Game

Objective
To combine word parts in order to recognize words and non-words

What the Research Says
"Readers of high and low proficiency use morphological cues to help them decode words" (Carlisle and Stone 2005).

Materials
- One set of cards for each group of students (provided on pages 25 and 26): prefix cards should be copied in one color, and ending cards should be copied in another color
- Chart paper for word and non-word chart

Directions
1. To introduce this game, copy and distribute the game cards to be used as a model activity. This game can be played individually, in pairs, or in a small group.

2. Each group of students needs one set of prefix cards and one set of ending cards. It's beneficial to copy the prefix cards in one color and the ending cards in another color.

3. To begin the game, one student turns over one prefix card. The other students, in turn, each turn over one ending card at a time. As each ending card is turned over, students determine if the term is a word or non-word and write the term on their chart under the appropriate column.

Word	Non-Word

4. Once students have used all of the ending cards with one prefix, a student turns over the second prefix card and students repeat the process of turning over the ending cards again to determine whether the terms are words or non-words. Students then write the words or non-words in the appropriate columns on their chart.

5. Depending on the time allowed in class, groups can stop after using one prefix or can do several or all of the prefixes provided.

6. Once students have finished, provide them with an answer key (on the next page) to check their words and non-words.

Answer Key for Creating Words Card Game

"un"	"pre"	"de"	"re"
unwind	preset	debrief	rewind
unset	prearrange	depart	reassign
unarmed	prebaked	deform	reform
unbaked	preview	decompose	recreate
	prepare	destroy	reset
	pretend	deconstruct	rearrange
		degenerate	rearmed
		denote	reverse
			review
			reconstruct
			regenerate
			respect

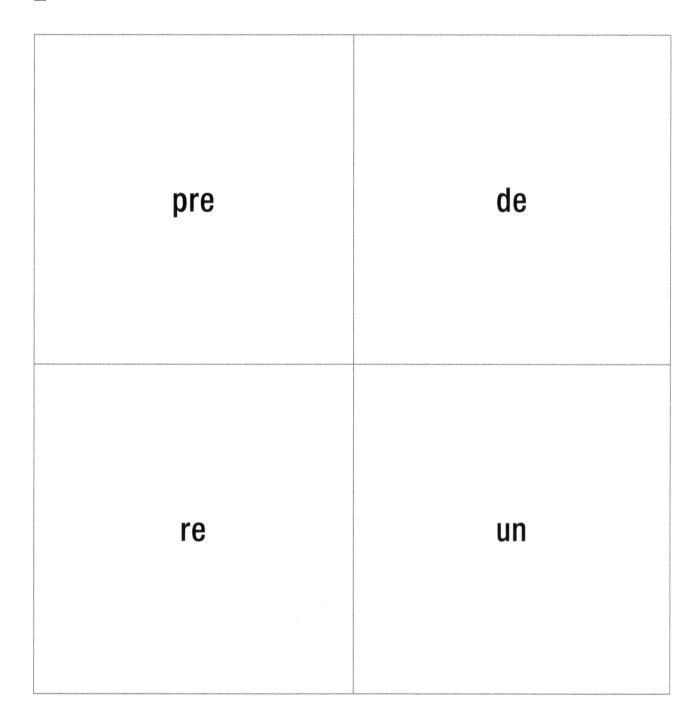

pre

de

re

un

wind	assign	brief	part
form	create	set	arrange
armed	compose	verse	stroy
baked	view	construct	pare
generate	tend	spect	note

Fluency Phrasing

COMMON CORE
STATE STANDARDS
Speaking and Listening 1

Objective

To see how stressing different words in a sentence affects how others perceive what is being read

What the Research Says

"For presentations at the middle-school level, students need to be able to select words and use tone that is appropriate to various situations and audiences" (Ryan and Frazee 2012).

Materials

"Fluency Phrasing" activity sheet (page 28)

Directions

1. On the document camera or Whiteboard, display the fluency phrasing model found on the next page.

2. Read the first sentence aloud to students, stressing the bold word, *I*. Ask students how stressing the word *I* impacts the sentence. They need to recognize that the person speaking wants to go to McDonald's. The speaker doesn't really care what anyone else wants; it's what the speaker wants.

3. Continue modeling the rest of the sentences, each with a different word stressed. Students need to be able to see that when stressing different words in a sentence, it can affect the tone and meaning of the sentence.

4. Share with students the next set of sentences. Have students explain how the bold word in each sentence affects the meaning of the sentence.

5. Next, instruct students to create their own set of sentences, highlighting one word in each sentence that will change the tone and affect the meaning of the sentence. Tell students that they will be sharing their sentences with the class.

6. Once students have completed their assignment, have several share their sentences aloud, reading them fluently while class members discuss the effect of the stressed word.

Fluency Phrasing Activity Sheet

Let's look at how the meaning of each sentence changes as the emphasized word changes.

Teacher Model: I do

I want to go to McDonald's.
(This means I want to go to McDonald's. I don't care about anyone else. I want to go there.)

I **want** to go to McDonald's.
(This means that I really, really want to go to McDonald's; there is no doubt in my mind.)

I want to **go** to McDonald's.
(This means that I want to physically go to McDonald's....no carry-out for me!)

I want to go to **McDonald's**.
(This means that I want to go to McDonald's and not Taco Bell, Burger King, or any other restaurant.)

Let's do one together: We do

Jamari can't get his locker opened.

Jamari **can't** get his locker opened.

Jamari can't get **his** locker opened.

Jamari can't get his **locker** opened.

Jamari can't get his locker **opened**.

Fluency Phrasing Activity

Now it's your turn to write a sentence where the meaning changes as different words are stressed. Write each sentence, underline the word to be stressed in each sentence, and then tell how the tone of the sentence changes with each different stressed word. Once completed, we will share these via the document camera or Whiteboard, or you will write your sentence on the board explaining how the stressed word affects the tone of each sentence.

Found Poems

COMMON CORE
STATE STANDARDS
Literature 1, 2, 4;
Informational Text 1, 2, 4;
Speaking and Listening 2, 4

Objective
To learn to select important facts and details in a text and arrange them to form a poem that is read fluently to a partner or the class

What the Research Says
"By intermediate grades, fluency no longer indicates comprehension. Many students can read all the words but are unable to talk about what they have read" (Routman 2003).

Materials
- Assigned text
- "Found Poem" critique sheet (pages 32 and 33)

Directions
1. This activity should be done upon completion of a fiction or nonfiction selection of text.

2. Upon completion of a reading assignment, students are directed to look for significant facts and details.

3. Instruct students to peruse the assigned text and take notes on profound or significant facts, details, phrases, and/or sentences in the text. If reading a fiction selection, students must locate at least one fact, detail, phrase, or sentence in each chapter. For a nonfiction text, students must locate one fact, detail, phrase, or sentence under each bold heading or section of text.

4. Once students have compiled a list of profound or important facts, details, phrases, and/or sentences, instruct them to arrange them to form a poem that flows. See the example from *Fahrenheit 451* by Ray Bradbury on the following page.

5. Once the poem is completed, students share by reading to a partner or to the class. Provide the listener(s) of the poem with a critique sheet (pages 32 and 33) to complete after the presentation of the poem.

6. Another way to present found poems is to have students present their poems in the form of a PowerPoint presentation with one fact, detail, phrase, or sentence on a slide along with an illustration. For this activity, not only are students practicing fluent reading, they are also gleaning information from the text.

Found Poem from *Fahrenheit 451* by Ray Bradbury

IT WAS A PLEASURE TO BURN.

Fire is bright and fire is clean.

He flicked the igniter and the house jumped up in a gorging fire that burned the evening sky red and yellow and black.

He felt the stars had been pulverized.

Right now I've got an awful feeling I want to smash things and kill things, 'take the beetle.'

The mechanical hound slept, but did not sleep, lived but did not live.

Miraculous bits of violet amber.

He saw himself in her eyes, suspended in two shining drops of bright water.

How can life be like this in the places we are?

The entire world was dark and gray.

The woman on the porch reached out with contempt to them all and struck the kitchen match.

Millie? Does the White Clown love you?

Does your family love you, love you *very* much, love you with all their heart and soul?

I often wonder if God recognizes His own son the way we've dressed him up, or is it dressed him down?

We have everything we need to be happy, but we aren't happy. Something is missing.

Nobody listens anymore.

It's not books you need, it's some of the things that once were in books.

The good authors touch life often. The mediocre ones run a quick hand over it. The bad ones leave it for the flies.

We are living in a time when flowers are trying to live on flowers, instead of growing on good rain and black loam.

That's the good part of dying; when you've nothing to lose, you run any risk you want.

Those who do not build them must burn.

What traitors books can be.

There was a crash like the falling parts of a dream fashioned out of warped glass, mirrors, and crystal prisms.

Give man a few lines of verse and he thinks he's the Lord of all Creation.

And then he was a shrieking blaze a jumping, sprawling, gibbering manikin.

There was a silence, and the silence was on the men's faces, and the time was there, time enough to sit by this rustling track under the trees and look at the world and turn it over with their eyes.

We're allotted a little space on earth and that we survive in that wilderness that can take what it has given.

Mildred, leaning anxiously, nervously, as if to plunge, drop, fall into that swarming immensity of color to drown in its bright happiness.

But every time he burnt himself up, he sprang out of the ashes; he got himself born all over again. And it looks like we're doing the same thing, over and over again.

And on the other side of the river was there a tree of life, which bare twelve manner of fruits, and yielded her fruit every month; and the leaves of the tree were for the healing of the nation.

Found Poem Critique Sheet

What did the presenter do to make this a fluent presentation?

_____

_____

_____

_____

Did the found poem flow smoothly? Did the presenter(s) speak clearly with appropriate rate and expression?

_____

_____

_____

_____

Were the facts presented in an organized manner that flowed with the topic? Give an example showing how the details in the poem illustrated the plot movement.

_____

_____

_____

_____

What information significant to the text was provided in this poem?

_____

_____

_____

_____

Tell something you learned from this poem that you didn't already know.

_____

_____

_____

_____

_____

_____

_____

_____

_____

_____

_____

_____

_____

_____

_____

_____

Four Flaps Graphic Organizer for Synonyms and Antonyms

Objective

To provide a synonym and an antonym for vocabulary words

What the Research Says

"A robust approach to vocabulary involves directly explaining the meanings of words along with thought-provoking, playful, and interactive follow-up" (Beck, McKeown, and Kucan, 2002).

Materials

One 8" square sheet of paper per student

Directions

1. Prepare a model as shown below to illustrate what students are required to do.

2. Provide each student with an 8" square sheet of paper. Students fold the paper from one corner to the opposite corner and crease. They then open the paper and fold it from the other corner to its opposite corner and crease. When opened up, the sheet has a plus sign in the center.

3. Students now fold each corner in to the center point. They now have a square with four flaps. Tell students to place their names on the back side of this graphic organizer.

4. Instruct students to select four vocabulary words and place one on the top of each flap. When they lift the flap, they place a synonym and an example on the opposite side of the word they wrote and an antonym and a non-example on the section below the synonym.

5. Display students' graphic organizers in the classroom for others to assess and view. Tell students that if they come across a synonym or an antonym that appears to be incorrect, they should let you know so it can be discussed further with the owner of the graphic organizer.

FIGURE 2

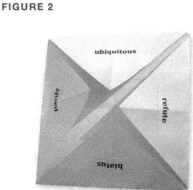

Frayer Model Paper Fold

COMMON CORE
STATE STANDARDS
Literature 1, 3, 4, 5;
Informational Text 4

Objective
To create four Frayer Models from one sheet of paper that can be used to play with words

What the Research Says
"Students represent the term in graphic form (reinforcing and deepening understanding through processing in a second modality)" (Marzano and Pickering 2005).

Materials
One sheet of 8 ½" x 11" paper for each student (notebook or copy paper)

Directions
1. Provide each student with one sheet of 8 ½" x 11" copy paper or a sheet of notebook paper.

2. Instruct students to fold the paper in half three times.
   1st fold: fold from the 8 ½" side to the other 8 ½" side
   2nd fold: with the fold on the top, fold from left to right (from one 5 ½" side to the other 5 ½" side)
   3rd fold: fold from top to bottom

3. Once the paper is folded, have students hold the paper with the folded spine on the left and the other folded section on top.

4. They then fold the top left corner over and crease.

5. They now open the paper and have two Frayer Model graphic organizers on each side of the paper. There is a diamond in the center with four sections on the outside.

6. There are several ways the graphic organizer can be used and arranged:
   a. Word in center, synonym, antonym, example, non-example
   b. Word in center, definition, illustration, personal connection, sentence
   c. Character's name in center, what the character looks like, how the character behaves, what others say about the character, what traits you like/dislike about this character

Variation
Instruct students to think of a word that belongs in the center of their graphic organizer but not to write it there. They then complete the other sections of the graphic organizer as they think of the word they are describing. Once students have their graphic organizers complete without the word in the center, collect all the papers. The next day, randomly pass out the papers, and have students read the descriptions and write the missing vocabulary word in the center of the graphic organizer.

GHOTI: Letters Don't Always Sound the Way They Look

Objective

To make students cognizant of the fact that letters do not always sound the way they look

What the Research Says

George Bernard Shaw once said that the word *fish* could be spelled *ghoti by* taking the *gh* sound from *enough*, the *o* sound from *women*, and the *ti* sound from *action*. The spelling for *fish* as *ghoti* may go back further to 1855. A publisher named Charles Ollier told a poet about his son's new spelling of *fish*: *ghoti*. This example shows that sometimes English spellings can be varied.

Materials

Board to write on or document camera

Directions

1. Write the word *ghoti* on the board.

2. Instruct students to decode this word. The first students to respond will call out *goaty*. Tell students that is not a word.

3. Tell students this is a word they will all be familiar with. Prompt them by telling them the *gh* takes on one sound, the *o* takes on another sound, and the *ti* takes on even another sound.

4. Allow students to work together to come up with words that have the *gh* sound, the *o* sound, and the *ti* sound.

5. If students do not come up with *ghoti* spelling *fish*, ask them to use the *gh* sound from enough, the *o* sound from women, and the *ti* sound from *action*.

   Now see who comes up with the word fish.

6. Ask students if they know any other letters or letter combinations that take on different sounds. Some examples to share might include the following:

   a. *ow* as in *cow*

   b. *ow* as in *show*

   c. *i* as in *wind* (turn)

   d. *i* as in *wind* (in the air)

   e. Long *a* can take on many letter representations:

      i. *ai* as in *rain*

      ii. *eigh* as in *sleigh*

      iii. *ay* as in *may*

      iv. *ai* as in *mail*

      v. *ea* as in *great*

   f. Long *e* can take on many letter representations:

      vi. *ea* as in *meat*

      vii. *ey* as in *key*

      viii. *y* as in *many*

      ix. *ie* as in *piece*

7. Challenge students to try to come up with unique spellings for common words as was done with *ghoti*.

I'm Going to...

Objective

To recognize beginning and/or ending sounds of words

What the Research Says

"The most common barrier to learning early word reading skills is the inability to process language phonologically" (Liberman, Shankweiler, and Liberman 1989).

Materials

- Soft item to throw (cushy ball, stuffed animal)
- "Beginning Sounds" and "Ending Sounds" exit slips (*next page*)

Directions

1. Introduce this lesson by explaining to students the difference between phonemes (sounds) and graphemes (letters). Examples: *phone* – the *ph* letters make the "f" sound; *made* – the ending letter is "e," yet the ending sound is "d"; *cat* – the beginning letter is "c," yet the sound it makes is "k."

2. Tell students that today they will listen for sounds only. You must decide if they will listen for beginning sounds (easy) or ending sounds, which is harder.

   You will select a location to take students on an imaginary journey, such as the mall, the zoo, a store, the woods, or someplace indigenous to your area. If you are focusing on beginning sounds, students will be eliciting words with the same beginning sound. Example: *I'm going to the mall to buy a tie*. The first student then throws the soft item to another person who must then use the "t" sound in *tie* to buy something else: *I'm going to the mall to buy a T-shirt*. Students continue throwing the soft item to others until no other students can think of something to buy at the mall beginning with the "t" sound. It's then time to change the beginning sound.

3. A more difficult variation of this game is to focus on ending sounds. Example: *I'm going to the mall to buy a shirt*. The next student must purchase something that begins with the "t" sound: *I'm going to the mall to buy a tie*.

   The next student must purchase something that begins with the "i" sound: *I'm going to the mall to buy ice cream*.

4. Topics can be changed at any time during the game.

Beginning Sounds Exit Slips

Use these exit slips after students have completed the "I'm Going to…" activity.

EXIT SLIP: Beginning sounds

Following the example below, use your name and tell what you like that begins with the same beginning sound as your name. You can use your first name or your last name.

Example: My name is <u>Jane</u>, and I like <u>jellybeans</u>.

You do: My name is _____ ,

and I like _____ .

Write your name here: _____

EXIT SLIP: Beginning sounds

Following the example below, fill in the blanks using words that begin with the same sound.

Example: I like to <u>dance</u> in the <u>desert</u>.

You do: I like to _____

        in the _____ .

Write your name here: _____

EXIT SLIP: Beginning sounds

Following the example below, fill in the blanks using words that begin with the same sound.

Example: I have a <u>cat</u> in my <u>kitchen</u>.

You do: I have a _____

in my _____ .

Write your name here: _____

EXIT SLIP: Ending sounds

Following the example below, fill in the first blank with any word and the second blank with a word that begins with the first word's ending sound.

Example: My name is <u>Jane</u>, and I like <u>nuts</u>.

You do: My name is _____ ,

and I like _____ .

Write your name here: _____

EXIT SLIP: Ending sounds

Following the example below, fill in the first blank with any word and the second blank with a word that begins with the first word's ending sound.

Example: I like to <u>read</u> in the <u>daytime</u>.

You do: I like to _____

in the _____ .

Write your name here: _____

EXIT SLIP: Ending sounds

Following the example below, fill in the first blank with any word and the second blank with a word that begins with the first word's ending sound.

Example: I have a <u>cup</u> in my <u>purse</u>.

You do: I have a _____

in my _____ .

Write your name here: _____

Knock-Knock Jokes Mini-book

Objective
To understand play on words

What the Research Says
"Word play is motivating and an important component of the word-rich classroom" (Blachowicz 2004).

Materials
- Knock-knock jokes (can be printed off the Internet or taken from books)
- One sheet of 12"x 18"white or light-colored construction paper per student
- "Knock-Knock Joke Peer Review" form (page 47)

Directions
1. Share with students several knock-knock jokes and discuss the play on words.

    Example: Knock, knock

    Who's there?

    Ice cream

    Ice cream who?

    Ice cream when I am at a concert.

    (*I scream*)

2. Now show students how you can change the ending of the joke:

    Knock, knock

    Who's there?

    Ice cream

    Ice cream who?

    Ice cream when I am mad.

    Knock, knock

    Who's there?

    Ice cream

    Ice cream who?

    Ice cream for my favorite team at the game.

3. Instruct students on how to create a mini-book using the **construction paper provided (see directions on page 73).**

4. Once their mini-book is made, students write the title of their book, *Knock-Knock Jokes*, on the front cover.

5. Explain to students that their task is to take a knock-knock joke and write the joke as they find it on the left-hand side of page one of their mini-book. On the right-hand side, they will rewrite the joke two times using a different ending each time. Tell students they can look at the jokes you have printed, in books if you provided any, or on the Internet. *Knock Your Socks Off: A Book of Knock-Knock Jokes* by Michael Dahl (Picture Window Books, 2010) is an excellent resource for this activity.

FIGURE 3

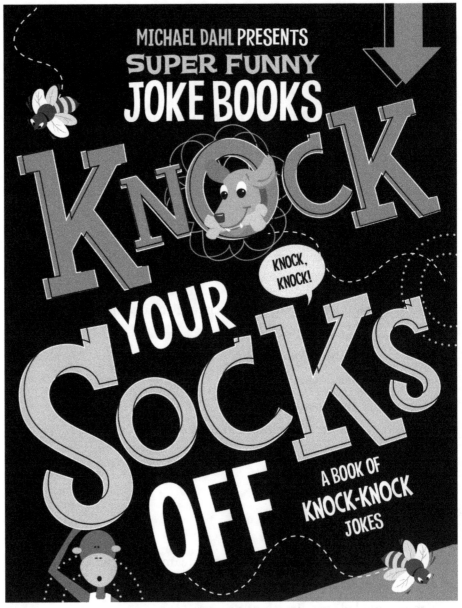

Knock Your Socks Off: A Book of Knock-Knock Jokes by Michael Dahl

6. Once students are done, allow them to trade joke books and complete the peer review form for each book they review. They will then return the form to the book's owner and review another.

Knock-Knock Joke Peer Review

AUTHOR: _____

1. Which joke in this book did you like the best?

   _____

2. What did you like about this joke?

   _____

   _____

3. Which joke(s) didn't you like? Why?

   _____

   _____

4. Provide a different ending to one of the jokes in this book. Write the
   joke with the new ending below.

   _____

   _____

   _____

   _____

   _____

   _____

   _____

   _____

   _____

   _____

   _____

   _____

   _____

Linear Array

COMMON CORE
STATE STANDARDS
Literature 4;
Informational Text 4

Objective
To distinguish the degree of strength in words

What the Research Says
"The linear array strategy can be used to demonstrate the connection between synonyms and antonyms by depicting the gradations between related words" (Allen 1999).

Materials
- Linear array words from list below
- Synonyms for "Big" handout (pages 50 and 51)
- Scissors
- Glue sticks
- Paper to glue words to (12" x 18" construction paper works well as do sheets of bulletin board paper)

Directions

1. Model for students the purpose of a linear array. Inform them that when writing, using strong vocabulary words can make a piece more powerful.
   - **Model:** This is a synonym/antonym array. It goes from sad to very happy.
     - Sad, depressed, melancholy, happy, joyous, thrilled, ecstatic
   - **Model:** This is a linear synonym array.
     - Fine, wonderful, fantastic, awesome, marvelous

2. Provide students with a copy of the "Synonyms for Big" handout (pages 50 and 51).

3. Instruct students to cut out the words and arrange them in a series that they believe goes from the weakest word to the strongest word.

4. Allow students to share their arrays. One student can place his words on the document camera. Another student can come up and rearrange the words in another order. Continue doing this, and discuss how there is no right or wrong answer, but you will probably notice that the "dull" words are often placed at the beginning of the array and the stronger words are often placed at the end of the array.

5. As a follow-up to this activity give the students a word from the list below and have them come up with their own arrays. Students should work independently to build their arrays. Then have students with the same word get together to share and discuss their work.
   a. Mad
   b. Great
   c. Awful

d. Fun

e. Sad

f. Pretty

g. Scared

h. Nice

i. Go

j. Make

k. Many

l. Cold

m. Hot

6. Another way to use linear arrays is to tell students to select one of their vocabulary words to create either a synonym/antonym or linear synonym array.

colossal	gigantic	huge
tremendous	large	gargantuan
immense	enormous	big
monstrous	massive	mammoth

COMMON CORE
STATE STANDARDS
Literature 1, 5, 10;
Informational Text 1, 5, 10

Making Predictions: An Activity with Movement

Objective

To make inferences and predictions about a selection by viewing isolated sentences from the selection

What the Research Says

"An introduction (to a book) generally sets up a frame for the whole story and often talks about the ending" (Calkins 2001).

Materials

Paper sentence strips with sentences or pieces of text from a selection written on them (example strips can be found on page 53)

Directions

1. Before beginning this activity with the students, the teacher must do one of the following:

    a. Copy a poem and cut it apart line by line into sentence strips. (Langston Hugh's poem, "Mother to Son," is an excellent poem to use for this activity.)

    b. Select lines of text from a reading selection, copy or print them, and cut them into sentence strips. The following pages contain lines from Rachel Hanel's book *The Japanese American Internment: An Interactive History Adventure*.

2. Distribute to each student one strip of paper that contains either one line of a poem or one sentence or chunk of text from a reading selection. Each student will receive a different line, sentence, or chunk of text.

3. Instruct students to get up and walk quietly around the room sharing their line, sentence, or chunk of text with others.

4. Once students have had the opportunity to read and share all of the lines and sentences, students return to their seats.

5. In small groups, allow students to make predictions about the selection to be read based on the lines or sentences they shared.

6. Once the group has had adequate time to discuss, allow each group time to share their predictions with the class.

7. Read the selection to determine if the predictions made when randomly viewing portions of the text were correct.

    a. If reading a poem, this activity can be completed in one class period.

    b. If reading a text selection, students will have to wait until the entire selection is completed before determining if their predictions were correct.

Example Sentence Strips

From *The Japanese American Internment: An Interactive History Adventure* by Rachel Hanel (2008), published by Capstone.

For more than two years, war has spread through Europe like wildfire. (pg. 7)

Yesterday morning, Japanese planes bombed American ships and planes at the Pearl Harbor military base in Hawaii. (pg. 7)

A large number of Japanese Americans live in California, Oregon, and Washington. (pg. 8)

But according to law, their parents and any others who came directly from Japan are not allowed to become citizens. (pg. 9)

The train takes you to the Manzanar camp in southern California. (pg. 13)

Eight guard towers anchor the corners of the camp. (pg. 14)

Row after row of barracks line the dirt streets. (pg. 15)

There are no chairs or tables in the apartment, only beds. (pg. 15)

You're not sure how much more of this camp life you can take. (pg. 31)

Joining the army would get you out of the camp right away. (pg. 31)

You graduate and move on to medical school in Chicago. (pg. 38)

After six days, you reach the soldiers. Many of them are dead. (pg. 39)

Japanese soldiers talk to each other in codes that you pick up on radio airwaves. Because of your training, you break their codes. (pg. 41)

The United States stays one step ahead of the Japanese and defeats them in 1945. (pg. 41)

All six of you share a space that used to be a horse stall. (pg. 43)

You are shocked by the lack of supplies. (pg. 48)

We were never allowed to become U..S. citizens. (pg. 50)

"The government's treatment is terrible and unjust. " (pg. 54)

On July 1, 1944, President Roosevelt signs Public Law 405. This law allows internees to give up their American citizenship. (pg. 61)

They say you are an enemy of the United States. (pg. 63)

Object Boxes

Objective

To recognize the number of sounds in a word

What the Research Says

"...the most effective way to teach children to read is through instruction that includes a combination of methods. The panel determined that effective reading instruction includes teaching children to break apart and manipulate the sounds in words (phonemic awareness)" (National Reading Panel 2000).

Materials

- One object box for each student, which can be copied from the "Object Box" template on page 57 or drawn on a sheet of paper;
- Objects to place in the boxes—scraps of paper, cotton balls, candy pieces, pennies

Directions

1. Provide each student with an object box or instruct students to copy an object box after viewing your model on the board or document camera.

2. Tell students that they will listen to a word and place one object that you have provided for them in each box to represent each sound they hear. **EXAMPLE:** For the word *dog*, students would place an object in three boxes: one for the "d" sound, one for the "o" sound, and one for the "g" sound.

3. It's a good idea for you to prepare a list of words in advance and separate the words into sounds. This makes for easy checking. Here's a list of words that might get you started with this activity:

- begin (5 sounds)
- meat (3 sounds)
- cry (3 sounds)
- baby (4 sounds)
- first (4 sounds)
- rain (3 sounds)
- peach (3 sounds)
- sheep (3 sounds)
- lamp (4 sounds)

4. As a challenge, ask students to determine the number of sounds in their own names. It's also challenging for them to determine the number of sounds in their vocabulary or word-wall words.

5. As a follow-up to this activity, instruct students to use a class reading assignment and locate three words that have three sounds, three words that have four sounds, and three words that have five sounds, and so forth. You can also challenge students to locate words with more than eight sounds. Use the Object Box for Word Sounds graphic organizer on the following page.

Object Boxes for Word Sounds

WORDS WITH 3 SOUNDS	WORDS WITH 4 SOUNDS	WORDS WITH 5 SOUNDS
WORDS WITH 6 SOUNDS	**WORDS WITH 7 SOUNDS**	**WORDS WITH 8 SOUNDS OR MORE**

Object Box Template

Picture It: Pictures to Words

Objective

To illustrate what pictures say in words

What the Research Says

"When children 'know' a word, they not only know the word's definition and its logical relationship with other words, they also know how the word functions in different contexts" (Stahl 2001).

Materials

- Pictures from calendars, magazines, photos, texts or art exemplars (can be found on the Internet)
- Sticky notes

Directions

1. This is a great activity to use with word wall words, especially when the word wall has a number of words, such as before a semester exam.

2. To model this activity, locate an illustration, such as an art exemplar. Using sticky notes, write one vocabulary word per sticky note and place it on the illustration. Explain to students how these words are a reflection of the illustration.

3. Have a variety of illustrations displayed around the room for students to view. If the illustrations are in a text, place the text open to the page on a desk, table, or countertop. Instruct students to walk around and view the illustrations, write vocabulary words on sticky notes, and place the sticky notes on the appropriate illustrations. Instruct students to write their initials or names on the sticky notes, so when you discuss the illustration and matching vocabulary words, the student(s) who wrote the word(s) can defend their position of what the word says about the illustration.

4. Once students have had sufficient time to complete the activity, discuss the illustrations and how the vocabulary words are a reflection of the illustrations.

Picture/Word Sort

COMMON CORE
STATE STANDARDS
K-5 Foundational Skills

Objective
To recognize beginning, ending, and vowel sounds in words

What the Research Says
"To become literate, the child must grasp the alphabetic principle—which means that the sounds we hear in words in English can be represented by written symbols" (Cooper, Chard, and Kiger 2006, 65).

Materials
- Magazines for students to cut out pictures
- Scissors
- Chart paper

Directions
1. Tell students that today they will be looking for pictures whose words contain various sounds. For example, students might have to locate pictures for words in the following categories:
   - words with long vowel sounds or short vowel sounds
   - words with an r-controlled vowel sound, such as "-or," "-er," or "-ur"
   - words with a hard "c," such as *cancer*, *plastic*, or *clown*
   - words with a soft "c," such as *city*, *circus*, *race*
   - words with a soft "g," such as *gas* or a hard "g," such as *gym*
   - words that begin with blends, such as "ch-," "sh-," "bl-," "br-," "cr-," "dr-," "cl-," "tr-," "st-," "gr-," "pl-," "fl-," "fr-," "sc-," "sk-," "str-," "sw-"

2. You must decide if students will work independently or in small groups and whether students will all focus on one sound or each group will work on a different sound.

3. Once students are in their groups, supply them with magazines, scissors, and chart paper. Instruct them to write their assigned sound on the top of their paper. They then cut out as many pictures as they can find that have their sound, either at the beginning, middle, or end of the word, and glue their pictures on their chart paper.

4. Charts can be displayed in the classroom.

SOFT "C" WORDS	LONG "A" WORDS	"CH-" WORDS

Raising Rigor: Questions at Different Cognitive Levels

Objective

To become familiar with question stems at different cognitive levels

What the Research Says

"It is critical that we craft lessons that move students to more challenging work while simultaneously providing ongoing scaffolding to support them as they learn" (Blackburn 2008).

Materials

- Fiction or nonfiction reading selection
- Sentence strips in three colors
- Question stems (pages 62 and 63)

Directions

Day 1:

1. After reading an assigned selection of text, provide students with the question stem suggestions on pages 62 and 63.

2. Provide each student with three sentence strips in three different colors (for example, one white, one blue, and one pink). Next, assign each student a number between one and the number of students in the class. Have each student write his or her assigned number on the three sentence strips.

3. The students' task is to write one question at each cognitive level. Low-cognitive-level questions will be written on one color sentence strip, medium-cognitive-level questions will be written on a second color sentence strip, and high-cognitive-level questions will be written on a third color sentence strip.

4. Once all of the questions have been written, provide students with an index card to write the answers to their questions. Instruct students to write the number that is on each one of their questions and the answer to their white, blue, and pink questions. This will be their answer key. Collect question strips and answer keys for use the following class period.

```
#18 white: answer
#18 blue: answer
#18 pink: answer
```

1. Place all of the low-cognitive-level (white) sentence strips together, and do the same for the medium-cognitive-level sentence strips (blue) and the high-cognitive-level sentence strips (pink).

2. Students can be required to answer all questions or be placed in groups according to their ability. Struggling students might be assigned only the low-cognitive-level questions (white sentence strips), while high-achieving students might be assigned only the high-cognitive-level questions on the pink sentence strips. Alternatively, students can each be required to answer a specific number of each type of question, such as five from each level.

3. Instruct students to take out a sheet of notebook paper. If they will be answering only one level of questions, they label their paper either "white" for the questions on white sentence strips, "blue" for the questions written on blue sentence strips, or "pink" for the questions written on pink sentence strips. If they are answering questions at all three cognitive levels, they can create three columns on their paper labeled "white," "blue," and "pink," or they can use three separate sheets of paper labeled "white," "blue," and "pink."

4. When done answering the questions, students check their answers. Place the students' answers in various places around the classroom. Answers one through five can be placed in one area, answers six through ten in another area, and so on. Students can then wander around the room checking their answers. Leave highlighter markers at each checking station to encourage students to highlight the questions they answered incorrectly for later discussion.

5. Once students have completed checking their answers, host a class discussion to review questions students had problems answering. Question strips can be placed on the document camera as you go over them.

6. Another way to review the questions is to have the question writers act as the experts. Each student will post a sign with his question number. Students who want to discuss the question can go to each expert's area.

Stems for Writing Questions at Low, Medium, and High Cognitive Levels

Low-Cognitive-Level Stems:
Bloom's Level 1 & 2—Remember and Understand

- Identify _____

- Define _____

- List _____

- Match _____

- Name all of the _____

- Who _____

- What _____

- When _____

- Where _____

- Illustrate _____

- Paraphrase _____

- What is the main idea of _____

- Give an example of _____

- Explain the reasons for _____

Medium-Cognitive-Level Stems:
Bloom's Level 3 & 4—Apply and Analyze

- Compare

- Contrast

- Interpret

- Do you know another time when _____

- Group by characteristics

- What would happen if _____

- Provide several opinions

- Provide several facts

- Categorize

High-Cognitive-Level Stems:
Bloom's Level 5 & 6—Evaluate and Create

- Summarize

- Apply

- Visualize

- Predict

- Infer

- Determine the author's point of view

- Pros and cons

- What would happen if _____

- How else might _____ have _____

- Construct

- Create

- How would you explain _____

Rap It Out

Objective

To learn content material by creating rap songs

What the Research Says

"One of the most desirable traits in the working world is the ability to communicate clearly and to work effectively as a team" (Allyn 2013).

Materials

Text to read

Directions

1. Upon completion of a text selection or novel, tell students that they will be putting the important details into a rap song.

2. Have students begin by creating a list of significant words or phrases in a selection.

3. Next, students must find words that rhyme with these words to use in their rap song.

   Example: The Industrial Revolution

   Was the evolution

   Of the problem of air pollution

4. The following rap was composed by a small group of students after reading a selection on a tsunami that hit Japan:

   Once upon a time not long ago

   A tidal wave came and swept the flo'

   Caused a real deadly quake shook the do'

   This wasn't a first in Kamaishi

   People were frightened thanks to another tsunami

   The students in the school were educated in class

   In case another tsunami would come to pass

   They researched its effect on the town

   To be prepared if once again it came around

5. Allow time for students to gather their words and ideas and write their raps. Let them know it's okay to write in small chunks as long as they are summing up the material they read. Several short raps can be as effective as one long one.

6. Allow each group to present their raps to the class. After each group presents, discuss with students the facts and information presented that were important to the text. Ask students what new information they learned from their peers' raps.

7. Raps can be exhibited on a "Rap It Out" display for students to view.

Reader's Theater with a Twist: From Prose to Play

Objective
To synthesize information in a narrative for a Reader's Theater play

What the Research Says
"Once you really pull in close to consider children's understandings (and their misunderstandings), it quickly becomes clear that 'simply' giving children time to read, texts they can understand, and conversations that hold them accountable to the text is a gigantic thing. An absolutely mind-blowing number of skills are needed and developed by anyone who reads with engagement and interest" (Calkins 2001).

Materials
- Narrative text to be rewritten as a play
- "Reader's Theater" comprehension question stems (page 68)
- "Reader's Theater" critique sheet (pages 69 and 70)
- "Reader's Theater" grading rubric (page 71)
- Paper and pencil

Directions

1. Before you begin this activity, you need to select several short stories, fables, or myths from your current literature text or other text that all students can access. Once you have selected the stories, you will have students turn them into Reader's Theater, creating a list of the characters in each selection.

2. Show a list of selections and characters in each selection on the board or document camera for all students to review. Provide time for students to look at the selections to determine which one they want to be a part of.

3. Once students have determined the selection they want to be a part of, have them write their names by the name of the character in the selection. When all characters have been chosen, you are ready to begin.

4. Provide students with the "Reader's Theater" grading rubric (page 71). Tell students their task is to turn the narrative into a play by writing a script that includes all of the important events in the plot. They will also create six comprehension questions to ask the audience at the end of their presentations. These questions should include two questions each at low, medium, and high cognitive levels. See page 68 for "Reader's Theater Comprehension Question Stems." Students will then present their Reader's Theater to the class. Costumes are not necessary, but props should be used to enhance the setting, characters,

and plot development. For example, if a sun is rising, a sun on a stick waved by a student would be appropriate. Stuffed animals, plastic snakes, hats, and glasses are simple props. There is no need for elaborate scenery.

5. Provide time in class for students to work in groups to write their scripts. This often takes several days. Each student must write his or her own speaking part. This is not a one-person operation!

6. Once scripts are written, allow time for students to practice. Two or three thirty-minute class sessions usually suffice. Students do not need to memorize their parts. In Reader's Theater, students are allowed to read from their scripts. You need to copy the final script so each student has a copy to read.

7. On the day of the performances, it's fun to set up a video camera and film the students' presentations. At the end of the school year, as you're winding down, students always enjoy watching themselves in action.

8. The show goes on with each group presenting their Reader's Theater, asking their comprehension questions, and having the audience complete the "Reader's Theater" critique sheet on pages 69 and 70.

Reader's Theater Comprehension Question Stems

Each group must write six questions for classmates viewing their play to answer upon completion of their presentation. Questions should include two low-level comprehension questions (Bloom's understanding and remembering), two medium-level questions (Bloom's applying and analyzing), and two high-level questions (Bloom's evaluating and creating).

Bloom's Low-Level Stems

Who?

What?

When?

Where?

Describe

Can you name all of the _____?

Paraphrase

Summarize

Bloom's Medium-Level Stems

Compare

Can you give another example of _____?

Tell how _____?

What conclusions can you draw?

What inference(s) can you make?

How did one character feel about another character? Explain.

Bloom's High-Level Stems

What were the consequences of _____'s actions?

How would you change _____?

What would have happened if _____ would have _____?

What are the pros and cons of _____?

What would have happened if _____?

Reader's Theater Critique Sheet

STORY PRESENTED:

_____

_____

GROUP MEMBERS:

_____

_____

1. Was the story plot clear? Write a brief summary of the story.

_____

_____

_____

2. A fluent presentation means speakers spoke with expression, proper intonation, and clarity.

   a. Which character(s) did an excellent job of speaking fluently?

   _____

   b. What did this character or these characters do that was exceptional?

   _____

   _____

   c. Which character(s) will need to improve in fluency?

   _____

   _____

   d. What do you think the character(s) mentioned above need to do to become more fluent?

   _____

   _____

3. Presentation includes eye contact and voice projection.

    a. Which character(s) did an excellent job with presentation?

    _____

    b. What did this character(s) do that was good?

    _____

    _____

    c. Which character(s) need to improve presentation style?

    _____

    d. What can the character(s) mentioned above do to improve presentation style?

Reader's Theater Grading Rubric

SELECTION TITLE: _____

STUDENT'S NAME: _____

GROUP MEMBERS: _____

_____

_____

_____ Worked well with group members; contributed to group effort   (20 points)

_____ Script was written with correct spelling and proper grammar—punctuation, sentence structure, and capitalization   (20 points)

_____ Script was written to illustrate highlights of the selection (20 points)

_____ Props were provided to enhance the characters, setting, and plot   (10 points)

_____ Six comprehension questions were written with two questions for each cognitive level—low, medium, and high (15 points)

_____ Presentation: part spoken fluently—projected voice, had proper tone, spoke at a reasonable rate (not too fast, not too slow)   (15 points)

_____ FINAL GRADE

COMMON CORE
STATE STANDARDS
Literature 10,
Informational Text 10

Reading Strategies Bookmark and Mini-book

Objective

To learn what reading strategies are and how to implement them while reading text

What the Research Says

"A skill becomes a strategy when the learner can use it independently, when she can reflect and understand how it works and then apply it to new reading material" (Robb 1996).

Materials

- Reading Strategies
- Bookmark (page 83)
- Two sheets of 12" x 18" or larger white construction paper per student
- One sheet of 6" x 9" construction paper per student
- One sheet of chart paper per student
- Several sticky notes per student
- Notebook paper, pens or pencils, highlighters, colored pencils or crayons

Directions

This activity will be done over a series of days.

"Making Connections" Strategy

Day 1:

1. Instruct students in making a "Reading Strategies" mini-book.

   a. Fold a sheet of construction paper in half, any direction, and make a good crease.

   b. Fold the paper in half once again, making a good crease.

   c. Now fold the paper one more time making a good crease.

   d. When you open the paper, you will have eight sections.

   e. Now fold the paper in half from the 12" side to the other 12" side.

   f. Cut the paper from the top center fold to the center.

   g. Now fold the paper in half from the 18" side to the other 18" side.

   h. Hold each 18" side in one hand, push, and then fold around to make the mini-book.

2. Provide each student with a copy of the "Reading Strategies" bookmark (page 83).

3. Instruct students to create the cover of their mini-book by writing the title "Reading Strategies" and illustrating.

4. Place the "Reading Strategies" bookmark on the document camera showing only the first strategy: "Making Connections."

5. Instruct students to copy the strategy name, "Making Connections," on the first page of their mini-book.

6. Discuss what is meant by making connections by providing examples of connections that are text to text, text to self, and text to world, using examples from a text read in class.

7. Instruct students to write a definition of making connections in their mini-book and provide an example of a text-to-text connection, a text-to-self connection, and a text-to-world connection from a selection read in class. They can also illustrate the page.

Day 2: Today students will practice making connections via dialogue with each other.

1. Arrange the classroom in small groups of four to six desks.

2. Each group of desks will have a card with one of the following titles:
   a. Video games
   b. Sports
   c. Books
   d. Television
   e. Shopping
   f. Music

3. Instruct students to take a seat at one of the groups of desks that has a topic of interest to them. If one group of desks is filled up, students must find a second choice.

4. Set an online timer, such as cooltimer.com, for approximately five minutes. Instruct students to make personal connections to the topic. As the facilitator, you will walk around the groups listening to conversations.

Day 3: Today students will practice making connections after reading a short selection.

1. Arrange the classroom in small groups of four to six desks.

2. Provide four to six copies of one short reading selection at each group. Each group will have a different selection to read.

3. Instruct students to take a seat at one of the groups of desks that has an article of interest to them. If one group of desks is filled up, students must find a second choice.

4. Provide time for students to read the article and make text-to-text, text-to-self, and text-to-world connections to the article read. Once again, walk around the groups listening in on conversations.

Day 4: Today students work independently to practice making connections.

1. Assign a short selection for students to read. This is a great opportunity to use a selection in a class text or a chapter of a novel the class is currently reading.

2. Once students have time to read the selection, have them write one text-to-text connection, one text-to-self connection, and one text-to-world connection.

3. Allow time for students to share what they have written.

"Questioning" Strategy

Day 1: **Students will understand the importance of questioning.**

1. Place the "Reading Strategies" bookmark on the document camera showing the strategy "Questioning."

2. Using an article, model the questioning strategy. Excellent articles can be found on the following websites: http://www.kellygallagher.org/resources/articles.html and http://www.englishforeveryone.org. An excellent resource for high-interest articles is *Texts and Lessons for Content-Area Reading* and *Texts and Lessons for Teaching Literature*, both by Harvey Daniels and Nancy Steineke.

3. Instruct students to write "Questioning" on the second page of their mini-book. Discuss why questioning is an important reading strategy and how asking questions can help clarify what is being read. Let students know that they should not be embarrassed to ask questions; often the questions they have are the same questions that others have.

4. Under the heading "Questioning" on page 2 of their mini-book, students will tell how asking questions helps them when they are reading a text. They can also illustrate the page.

Day 2: **Students will work collaboratively to practice questioning the text.**

1. Place students in small groups. Provide students with an article of interest to read. Each group will read the same article. The resources mentioned in Day 1, Step 2 provide excellent articles for students to read.

2. Provide each group with chart paper. Instruct students to write down questions they have as they read the article. If their questions are answered as they continue their reading, they are to write the answers as they find them.

3. Once each group has completed their reading and generated their questions, hold a class discussion for each group to share its questions. Questions not answered should be discussed.

Day 3: **Students will practice the turn-and-talk strategy to share questions with a peer.**

1. Model the turn-and-talk strategy to the students.

2. Assign a selection for students to read. Provide students with sticky notes.

3. Tell students that they will be reading a selection of text independently and writing their questions on sticky notes to be placed in the text where their questions occur.

4. When students have completed their independent reading, have them turn and talk to a partner, comparing questions and locating answers to their questions.

5. When students are done with their turn-and-talk, hold a class discussion to answer any questions that remain unanswered.

Day 4: **Students will practice the questioning strategy independently.**

1. Assign a selection or section of text for students to read. Students can all read the same selection or section of text, or students can choose a section in their text.

2. Instruct students to fold a sheet of notebook paper in half from left to right. They will label the left side "Questions/Page Number" and the right side "Answers/Page Number."

Questions/Page Number	Answers/Page Number

3. Students will read their text, noting questions they have about the text on the left side of their paper. They will also note the page number where the question arose. As they encounter the answer, they will write it on the right side of the page along with the page number where the answer was found.

4. When students have completed their reading, if they have questions that are unanswered, they must go back and re-read their text to try to locate the answers.

5. If students are all reading the same text, call the class together to discuss lingering questions. If students are reading different selections, they can be grouped by selection or the teacher can facilitate and assist with questions that are unanswered.

"Visualizing" Strategy

Day 1: **Students will understand the benefit of turning what is read into a picture.**

1. Instruct students to turn to the next free page in their "Reading Strategies" mini-book. Students will copy the definition of "visualizing" from the bookmark placed on the document camera.

2. Using a piece of text, model the visualizing strategy.

3. Have students write down how visualizing helps them when reading and then illustrate the page.

Day 2:

1. Place students in groups of four, five, or six, depending upon the number of students in the class.

2. Assign each group one chunk of text to read. This can be one or more pages or one section of text.

3. Tell students to read their chunk of text and then create an illustration of what they "saw" in the text.

4. Allow students to share their illustrations.

Day 3:

1. Assign a selection of text for students to read independently.

2. Once the reading is completed, instruct students to fold a sheet of construction paper into eight sections. They will do this by folding their paper in half three times. They are then to construct a storyboard showing what they read in picture form.

Day 4:

1. Provide each student with one 6" x 9" piece of construction paper. Assign a selection of text for students to read independently.

2. Instruct students to visualize the main idea of what was read and then illustrate the idea.

"Using Print Conventions" Strategy

Day 1: Students will understand the importance of print conventions.

1. Instruct students to turn to the next free page in their "Reading Strategies" mini-book. Students will copy the definition of "print conventions" from the bookmark placed on the document camera.

2. Have students write how being aware of print conventions assists them when reading.

Day 2:

1. Model for students by showing them what the print conventions are in a piece of text—key words, bold print, italicized words, punctuation, capital letters, sentence structure, charts, graphs, and illustrations— and discuss how these print conventions add to the text.

2. To make students aware of print conventions, select a piece of text to use as a model for a guided reading lesson. As you read to the students, stop at various places and point out the print conventions.

Day 3:

1. Provide students with a copy of text that includes print conventions like key words, bold print, italicized words, punctuation, capital letters, sentence structure, charts, graphs, and illustrations. Instruct students to highlight or underline all print conventions. If students cannot write on the text, instruct them to copy all print conventions on a sheet of paper. This activity allows students to interact with the text.

2. Place students in small groups to discuss the various types of print conventions they located. Have each student in the group compile a list of how these print conventions assisted them with their reading. As the facilitator, you will walk around listening to each group's discussions.

3. Each group member will share at least one item from their list with members of the group.

"Retelling" Strategy

Day 1: Students will understand that when they can retell what they have read, they understand what they have read.

1. Instruct students to turn to the next free page in their "Reading Strategies" mini-book. Students will copy the "retelling" definition from the bookmark placed on the document camera.

2. Students will then comment on whether or not they ever retell what they've read. If so, ask them to explain how and what they do to retell; if not, emphasize the importance of retelling to aid comprehension.

Day 2: Model the retelling strategy by reading a brief text selection to students and then retelling it to them.

Day 3:

1. Place students in pairs. Provide each pair with a selection of text. This can be a paragraph, a larger chunk of text, or an entire short story.

2. Instruct each student to read the text. Students can take turns reading aloud if they want. They are then to retell to each other what they read. Students must realize that because they both read the same text, they will be retelling similar information, yet each student will retell in their own words.

Day 4:

1. Provide students with a text selection. Instruct students to read the text and then retell what they read by either recording their retelling into their cell phone (see page 93), recording on a classroom computer via an online program like Audacity (http://www.audacity.sourceforge. net), or retelling to another student in the classroom. Students who record on their cell phones can send their recording to another student's cell phone. Students who record using Audacity can download another student's recording and listen to it via the computer or on their iPod. Each student should listen to another student's retelling.

"Re-reading" Strategy

Day 1: Students will understand that re-reading is done by even the best readers to help clarify confusing passages.

1. Instruct students to turn to the next free page in their "Reading Strategies" mini-book. Students will copy the definition of "re-reading" from the bookmark placed on the document camera.

2. Have students write down how re-reading the text helps them clarify.

Day 2:

1. Using a brief passage from your current text, model reading the text using the "think-aloud" strategy. As you have a question, write it on the board for students to see.

2. After reading the passage one time, tell students you are going to re-read it to clarify and try to answer the questions you had as you did the think-aloud.

Day 3:

1. Provide students with a brief chunk of text or a passage to practice the re-reading strategy. Students reading at different grade levels can be provided text at their appropriate reading level. Instruct students to write questions they have during their first read.

2. Tell students they will then read the text a second time to see if they can answer the questions they had. Instruct students to write their answers, if found, under or opposite the question(s) they wrote.

3. Provide time for students to share their questions and answers. Tell students that implementing the re-reading strategy can help them better comprehend text.

Day 4:

1. Share with students the "Re-reading Strategy Graphic Organizer" activity found on page 84.

2. Following the directions for the graphic organizer, students will create a "Re-reading Graphic Organizer" using a selection from your current text.

"Adjusting Your Reading Rate" Strategy

Day 1: Students will understand that each individual must read at a rate that is comfortable in order to obtain comprehension and that it's not a bad thing if you read slowly in order to comprehend.

1. Instruct students to turn to the next free page in their "Reading Strategies" mini-book. Students will copy the definition of "adjusting your reading rate" from the bookmark placed on the document camera.

2. Model reading an easy passage to students. Once you have read the passage, summarize or note the important details of what you read to show students that when the text is an easy read, comprehension comes easily.

3. Next, read a more difficult text to the students. Ask students to summarize or note the important points of what you read. Then re-read it at a slower pace and have students summarize or note the important points.

Day 2:

1. Select a passage from a text you are reading or distribute a reading selection to the students. Ask for a volunteer to read it aloud to the class at a fast pace. Have several comprehension questions ready for students to answer and instruct students to answer the questions after the reading.

2. Ask another volunteer to read the passage at a slower pace. Once again, instruct students to re-address the questions.

3. Discuss with students which reading pace made it easier for them to comprehend the text.

Day 3:

1. Provide students with an easy passage to read and several comprehension questions to answer.

2. Ask students if they had to re-read the passage or adjust their reading rate to answer the questions.

Day 4:

1. Provide students with a more difficult passage to read and several comprehension questions to answer.

2. Ask students if they had to re-read the passage or adjust their reading rate to answer the questions.

3. At this point, make students aware of the fact that adjusting their reading rate is necessary when they feel the text is difficult. Explain that reading rate will be different for each individual, and this is okay.

I Read It, But I Don't Get It
Cris Tovani (Stenhouse, 2000)

READING STRATEGIES:
A Bookmark

(to help when you "read it but don't get it")

Make connections between the text and your life:
Using knowledge to make a connection will help you understand your reading better.

Make a prediction:
Think about what's to come.
When an event doesn't match a prediction, rethink and revise your thinking.

Stop and think about what you've read:
Connect newly acquired knowledge with information you already have.

Ask questions:
Ask questions as you read.
Continue reading to find the answers.

Write about what you read:
Jotting down a few notes helps clarify meaning.

Visualize:
Create images in your head to help you make sense of what the words are saying.

Use print conventions:
Key words, bold print, italicized words, capital letters, and punctuation can all be used to enhance understanding.

Retell what you've read:
Ask yourself, "What have I just read?"
This helps refresh your memory.
Retelling is also helpful when returning to reading after some time has passed.

Re-read:
Re-read to help you understand the selection better.

Notice patterns in text structure:
Recognizing how a piece is organized helps you locate information more quickly.

Adjust your reading rate – slow down or speed up:
Good readers don't read everything fast.
Slow down when something is difficult.
Read faster when something is familiar.

COMMON CORE
STATE STANDARDS
Literature 1, 2, 3, 4, 6;
Informational Text 1, 2, 3, 4, 5, 6

Re-reading Strategy Graphic Organizer

Objective
To allow students to monitor their comprehension

What the Research Says
"When meaning breaks down, readers can stop and decide whether there is something in the text they can re-read that will help them understand the piece better" (Tovani 2000).

Materials
- One sheet of 8½" x 11" paper per student
- Reading selection

Directions

1. Instruct students to create the graphic organizer below by folding one sheet of 8½" x 11" paper from one 11" side to the other 11" side. Students will then divide the paper equally into three sections and cut the top section from the bottom to the top fold.

2. Students will then label each section: section one—"1st read," section two—"Turn and talk," and section three—"2nd read."

1st read	Turn and talk	2nd read

3. Assign students a text selection to read. Instruct them to take notes *in their own words* under the "1st read" section. Students can write questions they have, jot down important details, or make notes on areas of confusion.

4. Once they have completed reading the selection one time, students turn and talk to a partner about their reading. Have them share their "1st read" notes, adding ideas from their partner that they might not have on their graphic organizer.

5. Once students have completed their turn-and-talk, instruct students to read the selection for a second time. This time, they will take notes in the "2nd read" section of their graphic organizer.

6. When students have completed their graphic organizer assignments, hold a class discussion on the selection and clarify any concerns students might have with the interpretation.

7. When the class discussion has come to an end, have students write their reaction to this selection on the back of the graphic organizer; providing at least three significant details from the selection.

Snowball Fight

Objective

To determine beginning, middle, and ending sounds in words

What the Research Says

"Interventions to improve phonological awareness abilities lead to significantly improved reading abilities" (Bradley and Bryant 1983).

"Students who learn phonics do better in all aspects of reading...than those who do not learn it" (Chall and Popp 1997).

Materials:

Notebook paper

Directions

1. After assigning partners, use words from your current vocabulary or word wall and instruct students to each write one word on a sheet of notebook paper.

2. Students then ball each sheet of paper up as if they are going to throw it away.

3. Instruct students to stand up. Tell students that when you say "go," they will have a "snowball fight" by throwing their balled-up paper at another person. Each student should end up with someone else's wad of paper. Remind students that this is an organized "snowball fight" and not a free-for-all!

4. Instruct students to open their crumpled paper and read the word written on it. They are then to determine the beginning sound, first vowel sound, and ending sound of the word. They are to read their word, telling the beginning sound, first vowel sound, and ending sound to their partner.

5. Once this first round is completed, students once again wad up their paper, and have another "snowball fight." Students again end up with someone else's paper and repeat the process of telling their partner the beginning, first vowel, and ending sounds in their word.

6. This activity can be repeated as many times as you desire.

7. As the facilitator in this activity, walk around the room listening to students' responses and intervening when necessary.

Syllable Patterns Mini-book

COMMON CORE
STATE STANDARDS
K-5 Foundational Skills

Objective

To become familiar with syllable rules to assist in decoding words

What the Research Says

"The goal in decoding is to get the unknown word into a word that makes sense and is in the student's vocabulary" (Bhattarya and Ehri 2004).

"Graphosyllable analysis helps adolescent struggling readers read and spell words." (Journal of Learning Disabilities)

Materials

- One 12" x 18" sheet of construction paper for each student in white or a light color
- Document camera or board
- "Syllable Patterns" teacher page (pages 91 and 92)

Directions

NOTE: This lesson can be done over several days or several weeks, choosing one rule per day with continuous reinforcement following or one rule per week with continuous practice following.

1. Instruct students to create a mini-book using one sheet of 12" x 18" construction paper (see page 73 for instructions to make the mini-book).

   Students will title the cover of their book "Syllable Patterns."

2. On page 1 in the book, instruct students to write the following statement:

   The number of vowels in a word determines the number of syllables in a word. Remember that two or more vowels together usually make one sound, and "y" counts as a vowel. The "e" at the end of a word is often silent.

3. Model several examples of this rule for the students:

   (Example: **conversatio**n – 4 syllables)

   (Non-example: **attitu**de – 3 syllables)

   (Example: **merrily** – 3 syllables)

   (Non-example: **o**bscure: 2 syllables)

   (Example: **dictiona**ry – 4 syllables)

   (Example: **E**gypt – 2 syllables)

   (Example: **sibling** – 2 syllables)

4. Instruct students to locate a word in a text they have for which they will need to determine the number of syllables. Have several students share their words and the number of vowel sounds and syllables.

5. Students should then prepare a chart on page 2 of their mini-book to record the number of syllables in words.

1	2	3	4	5	6

Provide a set amount of time (5–10 minutes) for students to locate as many words as they can for each number of syllables and place their words on their charts. Allow time for sharing on the document camera or board.

CVC Rule

1. On page 3 in the mini-book, students write "CVC: short vowel rule." Students will write, "The rule states that when you have the CVC pattern, the vowel sound is short."

2. Provide several examples of this rule: "cat," "dog," "mud," etc., and let students know that several CVC syllables can be combined to form longer words: "carpet," "farthest," "pommel," "tempest," "helmet," "dismiss," "kitten," "garlic," "gastric."

3. As a group, students skim over a text selection to locate and share words with the CVC pattern.

4. Instruct students to locate four more words with the CVC pattern and write them in their mini-book. Allow time for students to share their findings.

CV Syllable

1. Page 4 of the students' mini-book will be labeled "CV syllable" where the vowel is at the end of the word: "be," "he," "go," "me," "no," "we."

2. Next, inform students that the CV can be added to a CVC to form many words:

    "nomad," "topaz," "lilac," "putrid."

3. Instruct students to locate one example of the CV or CV + CVC rule in the text they are using and share it with the class.

4. Now, students must each locate several CV or CV + CVC words and write them on page 4 of their mini-books. Provide time for students to share their findings.

Cle Syllable

1. Page 5 of students' mini-book will be labeled with "Cle syllable" and the definition: "This is only used as a final syllable in a word."

2. Provide several examples of this rule: "bicycle," "tricycle," "giggle," "tickle," "pickle."

3. Allow students to peruse their text to locate other words that end with the Cle syllable.

4. Now, instruct students to independently locate several Cle words in their current text material and write these words on page 5 in their mini-book.

r-Controlled Syllable

1. Page 6 of the students' mini-book will be labeled "r-Controlled Syllable," defined as a combination of one of the following: /ar/, /er/, /ir/, /or/, or /ur/.

2. Share with students three different sounds made by the r-controlled syllable: 1. /ar/, 2. /or/, and 3. /er/, /ir/, and /ur/, which all make the same sound. Sound out these syllables for the students.

3. Provide several examples of the r-controlled syllable:

   /ar/: "car," "far," "bar," "tar," "mar," "cart," "dart," "start"

   /or/: "for," "more," "tore," "store," "floor"

   /er/, /ir/, /ur/: "fern," "fir," "fur," "during," "turn"

4. Have students in groups elicit words with the r-controlled syllable. They can peruse their current text to locate words.

5. Now, instruct students to locate several words with the r-controlled syllable and write them on page 6 of their mini-book.

CVCe Syllable

1. Page 7 of students' mini-book will be labeled "CVCe Syllable." Instruct students to write the following definition: "This rule states that when a word ends with a CVCe syllable, the vowel sound will be long."

2. Provide several example words with the CVCe syllable: "make," "ride," "divide," "hope," "cube," "impose."

3. Have students look through their current text to locate examples of words with the CVCe syllable and share their findings.

4. Instruct students to locate several CVCe words in their current text and write these words on page 5 of their mini-book.

CVVC Syllable

1. Page 8 of students' mini-books will be labeled "CVVC Syllable" with the following definition: "This syllable pattern often sports the jingle 'when two vowels go a-walking the first one does the talking'."

2. Provide students with several words with the CVVC syllable: "boat," "goal," "receive," "train," "daisy," "people."

3. Have students look through their current text to locate examples of words with the CVVC syllable and share their findings.

4. Instruct students to independently locate several words with the CVVC syllable in their current text and write these words on page 8 of their mini-books. Allow time for students to share their findings.

For more activities, mini-lessons, guided practice, and games using syllable patterns, see *Teaching Syllable Patterns: Shortcut to Fluency and Comprehension for Striving Adolescent Readers* by Lin Carver and Lauren Pantoja (Maupin House, 2009).

Syllable Patterns Teacher Page

This page is to be used on the document camera when introducing syllable patterns; this is what the students write on each page of their mini-books.

Mini-book Cover: Label as "Syllable Patterns"

Page 1: The number of vowels in a word determines the number of syllables in that word. Remember that two or more vowels together usually make one sound, and "y" counts as a vowel. The "e" at the end of words is often silent.

Page 2:

1	2	3	4	5	6

Page 3: CVC: short vowel rule
Locate 4 words with the CVC pattern. Write them on this page.

_____

_____

_____

_____

Page 4: CV: a vowel at the end of a word will be long
Locate 4 words with the CV pattern. Write them on this page.

_____

_____

_____

_____

Page 5: Cle: used as a final syllable

Locate 4 words with the Cle pattern. Write them on this page.

_____

_____

_____

_____

Page 6: r-controlled syllable: (/ar/, /or/, /er/, /ir/, /ur/)

/ar/ is one sound; /or/ is another sound; and /er/, /ir/, /ur/ make the same sound.

Locate 4 words with the r-controlled vowel sound. Write them on this page.

_____

_____

_____

_____

Page 7: CVCe: When, at the end of a word, the vowel sound will be long.

Locate 4 words with the CVCe pattern. Write them on this page.

_____

_____

_____

_____

Page 8: CVVC: When two vowels go a-walking, the first one does the talking.

Locate 4 words with the CVVC pattern. Write them on this page.

_____

_____

_____

_____

Using Cell Phones and Audacity to Become a More Fluent Reader

COMMON CORE
STATE STANDARDS
Speaking and Listening 2, 6

Objective
To hear oneself and others read aloud

What the Research Says
"The best strategy for developing fluency is to provide your students with many opportunities to read the same passage orally several times" (Armbruster and Osborn 2001).

Materials
- Appropriate leveled text
- Cell phone or Audacity (it's free) loaded on computer. A microphone is needed if one is not built into the computer.
- MP3 player or iPod (convenient but not necessary)
- "Fluency Playback" critique sheet (pages 94 and 95)

Directions
1. Provide students with reading material; this can be a paragraph, passage, or short story.

2. Cell phone: If the student has a cell phone, this activity is as simple as recording the reading into their cell phone. Depending on the cell phone, students can make a voice recording using one of these apps: utilities, voice search, voice command, sound recorder, or voice recorder.

3. Audacity: If the student will be recording on the computer, download Audacity for free at http://audacity.sourceforge.net. Once into Audacity, the student clicks the "record" button. The student can then rewind to the beginning and play it back. It's that simple!

4. Once the student has finished recording with a cell phone or Audacity, instruct him or her to complete the "Fluency Playback" critique sheet (following page) while listening to their recording.

5. Students can also critique each other. Students using their cell phones can send their recording to another student via email. Students using Audacity can listen to another student's file on the computer or download the file onto an MP3 player or iPod. Students critiquing each other should have a copy of the text they are reviewing.

Fluency Playback Critique Sheet

PERSON RECORDING: _____

PERSON CRITIQUING: *(if self, write "self")* _____

1. Recorder spoke clearly; I was able to understand what he or she was saying.

    YES   NO

    If you circled **NO** above, what could the recorder do to be understood better?

    _____

2. Recorder spoke with expression; I noticed different pitches in his or her voice.

    YES   NO

    If you circled **NO** above, what does the recorder need to do to better his or her expression?

    _____

3. Recorder read with proper phrasing; he or she stopped or paused when punctuation was present.

    YES   NO

    If you circled **NO** above, where did the recorder not stop?

    _____

4. Recorder was able to recognize words automatically; he or she did not spend a lot of time trying to figure out how to say a word(s).

    YES   NO

    If you circled **NO** above, what words did the recorder struggle over?

    _____

5. Provide a brief summary of the selection you critiqued.

_____

_____

_____

_____

_____

_____

_____

_____

_____

_____

_____

_____

_____

_____

COMMON CORE
STATE STANDARDS
Literature 1, 2, 3, 4, 5, 6

Using Tunes to Teach Literary Elements

Objective

To recognize that song lyrics are poetry that send a message using figurative language

What the Research Says

"If students are to understand what they read, then teachers must find text that they can read to supplement the textbook—as well as give them time to practice new strategies for understanding the reading during class time" (Tovani 2004).

Materials

- Song lyrics printed out for each student
- Song to listen to (CD or download)

Directions

1. Distribute song lyrics to students.

2. Instruct students to follow printed lyrics as they listen to the song. You can play a CD or find the song (and often the lyrics) on the Internet or YouTube.

3. Replay the song; instruct students to underline figurative language (similes, metaphors, onomatopoeia, personification, hyperbole) as they listen to the song.

4. Divide students into small groups and then follow either (a) or (b):

   a. Assign each group one stanza.

   b. Assign each group the entire song lyrics.

      Whether focusing on a stanza or entire lyrics, each group is to interpret their lines, locate the figurative language, and explain it. Students must also interpret their assigned stanzas.

5. Each group should be prepared to read their stanzas to the class, discuss the figurative language in the stanzas, and explain what the writer is saying.

A NOTE: Students love this activity. Encourage them to print out their favorite lyrics for interpretation. Of course, you will have to read prior to copying and distributing to assure clean content. My students enjoyed this activity so much that they were bringing me lyrics and CDs of their favorite songs and begging me to do this activity more often.

Viewing Movies: A Graphic Organizer for Fiction and Nonfiction

COMMON CORE
STATE STANDARDS
Literature 1, 2, 3, 6, 7;
Informational Text 1, 2, 3, 6, 7

Objective

To teach literary elements through listening and viewing

What the Research Says

"Listening is half of the oral language pair. When we listen, we receive and make sense of the oral language of others. Listening is *receptive oral language*." "There is only a fine line between gaining meaning from regular language-type print and other material that is printed and/or viewed." "Viewing, then, is a receptive language arts skill." (Kasten et al. 2005).

Materials

- Movie DVD
- Note-taking graphic organizer (see "Movie-Viewing Graphic Organizer for Fiction" and "Video-Viewing Graphic Organizer for Nonfiction" on pages 98 and 99)

Directions

1. Provide each student with a movie note-taking graphic organizer for either fiction or nonfiction (pages 98 and 99).

2. Before watching the movie see if you can find a movie trailer on the Internet, then allow students to complete the "before viewing" section.

3. Review the graphic organizer with the students before beginning the movie.

4. Instruct students to fill in the graphic organizer as they view the movie. They can write on the back of the graphic organizer if they run out of room on the front.

5. After viewing, students can meet in small groups to discuss their responses.

6. Via class or small-group discussion, allow students to share the information on their graphic organizers.

7. If viewing a movie of a book read in class, instruct students to create a Venn diagram comparing the book and the movie.

Movie-Viewing Graphic Organizer for Fiction

Before viewing: If there is a movie trailer... What were you thinking as you watched this movie trailer?	**Before viewing:** If there is no movie trailer... What does the title tell you about this movie?
While watching the movie, what **conflicts** arose? Circle the major conflict. Tell how each conflict was resolved.	What was the main **setting** in the movie? How did this setting contribute to the story?
Select one **character** in this movie. Describe his or her personality by providing examples of what the character says and does and what others say about them. Provide specific examples.	Provide a list of important **details** in the plot.
What was the **theme** of this movie?	On the back of this graphic organizer, write a **movie review**.

Video-Viewing Graphic Organizer for Nonfiction

Before viewing:	Before viewing:
Topic _____ What **do** you know about this topic?	What **don't** you know about this topic?
What questions did you have while watching the video?	What questions did you have that were not answered in the video?
While watching the video, what facts did you already know?	What did you learn while watching this video?
Create a visual of an important fact seen in the video.	How did what you saw in this video compare to information read in your text? What information was new? Was any information repeated?

Vocabulary 8-Squares

Objective
To make personal connections to a fiction or nonfiction selection

What the Research Says
"Vocabulary knowledge is one of the five essential components of effective reading" (RAND Reading Study Group 2002).

Materials
- One sheet of 8½" x 11" paper or notebook paper per student
- List of vocabulary words or word wall of words
- Box, bag, or basket to collect the word cards students are creating
- "Vocabulary 8-Squares" critique sheet (page 102)

Directions
1. After reading a selection of fiction or nonfiction, students take their sheet of paper and fold it in half three times. When they open the paper, they will have eight sections.

2. Students then label each section: 1—Color; 2—Person; 3—Place; 4—Music; and 5, 6, 7, and 8—Vocabulary word. See below:

Color	Person
Place	**Music**
Vocabulary word	**Vocabulary word**
Vocabulary word	**Vocabulary word**

3. In the box marked "Color," students write a color they thought about as they read their selection. In the box marked "Person," they write the name of a person they thought about as they read their selection. In the box marked "Place," they write the name of a place they thought of as they read their selection. In the box marked "Music," they write the type of music that would be appropriate to listen to as they read this selection. And in each box marked "Vocabulary word," they are to write one of their vocabulary words.

4. Once students have filled in each section, instruct them to cut the eight sections apart and place them in the box, bag, or basket you provided for them.

5. Next, pass the box, bag, or basket around and instruct students to take out the same number of pieces they put in (usually eight per student).

6. Tell students they can work independently, in pairs, or in small groups. Their task is to use all of their words to create a story. This story can, but does not have to be related to the theme of the selection read. Students working independently will have eight words to incorporate into their story. Students working in pairs will have sixteen words, and students working in small groups will have eight words for each person in the group. Of course, there is a chance that students will have duplicate words; these words will only get used once.

7. Once students have completed their stories, they can share orally with the class or pass their stories around the room for each student, pair, or group to read. The critique sheet on the following page can be used for students to critique each other's stories.

Model based on *Deadly Invaders* by Denise Grady (Kingfisher, 2006)

Words from graphic organizer: color–red; person–doctors; place–Angola; music–blues; vocabulary words–infectious, virus, contagious, antibiotics

In the country of Angola, there is an infectious disease going around. Everyone is angry. It's causing everyone in the country to see red. The virus is very contagious. Doctors do not have antibiotics for it. There is no cure. Many people need to wear helmets and jackets so they don't breathe it in or get it on their skin. A cure is needed as soon as possible. Many people get the blues when they get this disease.

Vocabulary 8-Squares Critique Sheet

STUDENT(S) WRITING THE STORY:

_____

_____

STUDENT(S) CRITIQUING THE STORY:

_____

_____

1. What did you like about the story?

_____

_____

_____

2. Was the story well organized? Did it flow? Did it make sense and have a beginning, a middle, and an end? _____ If not, can you make suggestions to organize the story better?

_____

_____

_____

_____

3. Was adequate support provided to develop ideas? _____ If yes, give an example. If not, what details could have been added to the story to make it more developed?

_____

_____

_____

4. Were the vocabulary words used effectively? Did they make sense the way they were used in the story? _____ If not, which word(s) were used ineffectively? How might they have been used more effectively?

_____

_____

_____

Vocabulary Graffiti Wall

COMMON CORE
STATE STANDARDS
Literature 4,
Informational Text 4

Objective

To share synonyms, antonyms, definitions, and parts of speech and to use words in sentences to show understanding of vocabulary words

What the Research Says

"Students learn words in a variety of ways" (Blachowicz and Fisher 2004).

Materials

- Large piece of bulletin board paper to create the graffiti wall (more than one vocabulary wall can be created)
- Pencils, pens, markers

Directions

1. Prepare one or more graffiti walls, providing one vocabulary word and the part of speech in each section of the wall.

FIGURE 4

Vocabulary Graffiti Wall		
scour verb D: clean S: scrub D: search S: comb A: dirty D: polish I had to scour the dinner dishes.	**subordinate** noun D: lower in rank S: assistant S: helper A: chief A: superior My goal in life is to be the head of a business not a subordinate.	**confiscate** verb D: to seize by authorities S: commander A: return A: restore S: expropriate The coast guard confiscated the ship's cargo.
refute verb D: to prove incorrect S: disprove A: prove S: rebut A confirm The teacher wanted me to refute the math problem.	**constrain** verb D: to hold back S: confine S: limit A: loosen A: relax S: pressure The officer had to constrain the prisoner.	**pacify** verb D: to make peaceful A: anger S: placate D: to soothe A: ignite My mom tried to pacify my baby brother, who was upset.

Vocabulary Graffiti Wall

2. Tell students this is a quiet activity. They are to add the following contributions to the chart:
   - Definitions: They will place the letter "D" by the definition(s) they contribute.
   - Synonyms: They will place the letter "S" by the synonym(s) they contribute.
   - Antonym: They will place the letter "A" by the antonym(s) they contribute.
   - Parts of speech: They will place "POS" by a different part of speech than what you originally put on the chart.
   - Sentences: Students contribute a sentence using a vocabulary word.

3. Students may contribute one or more items, and they do not have to contribute in all squares.

4. When the wall has been completed (this can be done on another day), you can assign one square to each student or pair of students who then become the expert(s) for that word. This expert makes sure that all of the components of the square are correct. Instruct students to write any discrepancies they find on a sheet of paper or an index card to share with the class. Students may also write questions they have if they are not sure the components of the square are correct.

5. Students can then place their papers with discrepancies on the document camera to share any errors or misunderstandings they found in their square.

Vocabulary Madness

COMMON CORE
STATE STANDARDS
Literature 4,
Informational Text 4

Objective
To analyze the importance of vocabulary words by comparing one word to another

What the Research Says
"When students are provided varied and frequent opportunities to think about and use words, it enhances their language comprehension and production and in the end, it affects reading comprehension" (Beck, McKeown, and Kucan 2002).

Materials
- Vocabulary words from word wall or text
- Blank "Vocabulary Madness" matrix (page 106)
- "Vocabulary Madness Rationale" sheet (page 108)

Directions
1. This activity works well when students work in pairs or small groups. It can be done in one or two days. Day one can be used to place the words on the matrix. The next day complete the rationale sheet.

2. Provide students with a list of vocabulary words, a blank "Vocabulary Madness" matrix, and a "Vocabulary Madness Rationale" sheet, found on the pages that follow.

3. Using the models provided for this activity, ask students to select any two words from their vocabulary list or word wall and place the words on the "Vocabulary Madness" matrix. The words can be placed in any order. Show the matrix model that has been provided.

4. Tell students that once they have their words on the matrix, they will need to think about the two words and determine which word they believe to be more powerful. They will do this by completing the "Vocabulary Madness Rationale" sheet; they must state which word "won" and why. Show students the rationale that has been provided as a model.

5. Once students have completed their matrices and rationale sheets, display in the classroom for all to view.

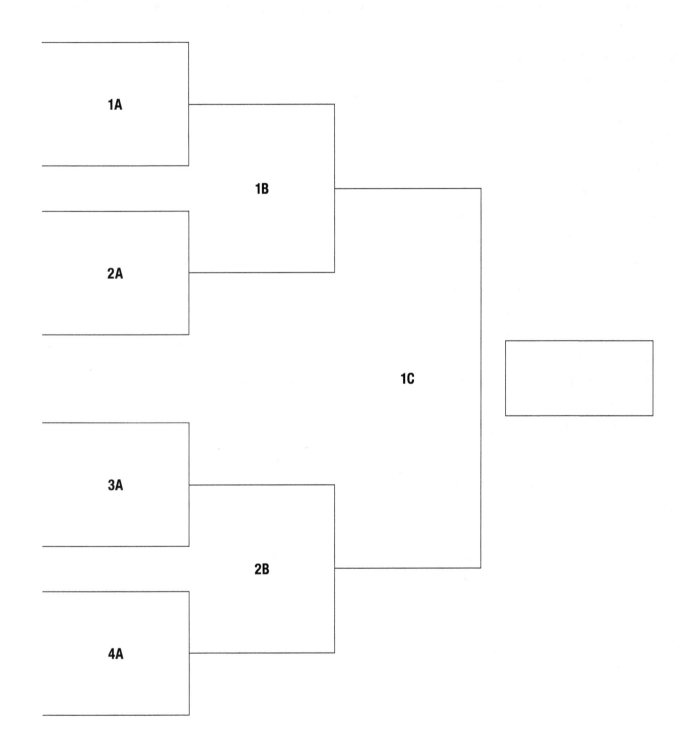

Vocabulary Madness Matrix Model

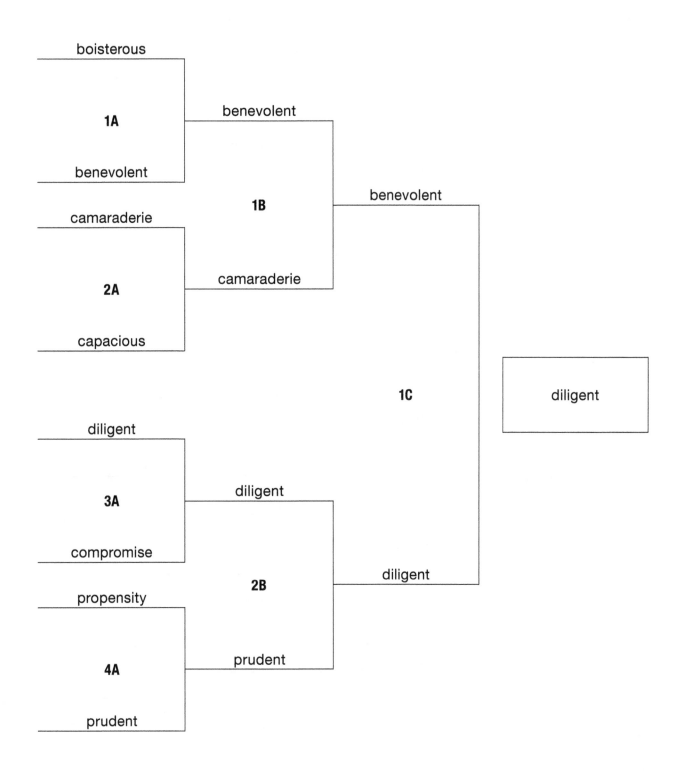

Vocabulary Madness Rationale

1A: _____ won over _____

because _____

_____

_____ .

2A: _____ won over _____

because _____

_____

_____ .

3A: _____ won over _____

because _____

_____

_____ .

4A: _____ won over _____

because _____

_____

_____ .

1B: _____ won over _____

because _____

_____

_____ .

2B: _____ won over _____

because _____

_____

_____ .

1C: _____ won over _____

because _____

_____

_____ .

Vocabulary Madness Rationale Model

1A: "Benevolent" **won over** "boisterous"
because being boisterous is not always a good characteristic while being benevolent is being able to be kind and caring.

2A: "Camaraderie" **won over** "capacious"
because when you have camaraderie, you do not need a lot of space, and if you do, your friends will give it to you.

3A: "Diligent" **won over** "compromise"
because being diligent will get you far in life, yet when you compromise yourself or your beliefs, you often give up something.

4A: "Prudent" **won over** "propensity"
because even though you might have a natural tendency toward something, it doesn't mean you are wise. I'd rather be wise than have a tendency to do something that might not be wise.

1B: "Benevolent" **won over** "camaraderie"
because you might have much camaraderie with the wrong people, like a group of friends that is not kind and caring. It's much more important to be kind and caring to everyone.

2B: "Diligent" **won over** "prudent"
because as far as I'm concerned, if you are diligent and stay on top of things, then you are prudent.

1C: "Diligent" **won over** "benevolent"
because benevolent people are kind and caring but not necessarily hard workers. I would rather be hardworking and conscientious than just kind and caring.

COMMON CORE
STATE STANDARDS
Literature 4,
Informational Text 4

Vocabulary Mini-book:
Different Cognitive Levels

Objective
To demonstrate comprehension of vocabulary words at different cognitive levels

What the Research Says
"Studies have shown that reading comprehension and vocabulary knowledge are strongly correlated" (Johnson and Johnson 2012).

Materials
"Vocabulary Mini-book" template (page 111)

Directions

1. Provide each student with a "Vocabulary Mini-book" template. Instruct students on how to fold the mini-book (see instructions on page 73).

2. Place slips of paper with vocabulary words in a basket or bag. Should you have more students than vocabulary words, duplicate some of the words or put review words from past lessons in the basket or bag. Pass the basket or bag around the classroom and ask each student to remove one word. This is the word the student will use to complete the mini-book. If students want to trade words, let them do so.

3. Place the mini-book template on the document camera. Discuss the various categories students will fill out for the vocabulary word. Allow time for students to complete their mini-books. Collect all completed mini-books and number them on the front cover.

4. The following day, instruct students to number a sheet of paper from one to the final number of mini-books. Then randomly pass a completed mini-book out to each student. Their task is to read through the definitions in the mini-books at the various cognitive levels and make a note on their notebook paper by the number of the mini-book they have as to which cognitive-level definition most helped them to learn this word.

5. Once each student has reviewed his or her first mini-book, he or she trades with another student and repeats the exercise, placing his or her answer by the number of each mini-book he or she reviews in the time allotted.

6. Continue until each student has had time to view several different mini-books and respond on their sheet.

7. The next day, call out a vocabulary word. Students write down the word and one thing they know about this word.

**One Word
Many Cognitive Levels**

My word _____

My name _____

Knowledge/Remember:

Define the word

Comprehension/Understand:

Write a definition in
your own words

Synthesis/Create:

Create a song, rap, or
cartoon using this word

Application/Apply:

Use the word in a
complete sentence

Evaluation/Evaluate:

Provide a linear array using your word

ex: big, huge, gigantic
everywhere, omnipresent, ubiquitous

Analysis/Analyze:

Provide an example
and a non-example

What's in the Bag?

Objective
To recognize the beginning, ending, and vowel sounds in words

What the Research Says
"Students who have excellent phonological awareness become better readers than those students who have poor phonological awareness" (Adams et al.1998).

Materials
One paper bag with common household/classroom items for each small group of three students:

plastic bag	headphones
cotton ball	book
playing cards	stapler
ball	fork
pen	spoon
tape	leaf
paper	dirt (in a plastic bag)
crayon	sock

Directions

1. Divide students into groups of three. If there are two extra students, they can form a group; if there is one extra student, pull one from a group of three to form a group of two.

2. Provide each group with a paper bag containing five or six items. The bags for each group can contain the same or different items.

3. Students pull one item at a time out of the bag. One student says the beginning sound of the item, another student says the first vowel sound, and the third student says the ending sound. During this activity, the teacher walks around the room as the facilitator and stops by each group to listen and clarify if needed.

4. If each group has a different bag of items, groups can trade with one another once they finish with their bag.

5. When you feel students have had sufficient time with this activity, hold several items up and have individuals tell the beginning, middle, and ending sounds heard in these words.

Word Pyramid

Objective

To see that when letters are added to a word or change position in a word, the sound the letter(s) make can change

What the Research Says

"Failure to master phonics or related word-analysis skills is easily the number one cause of reading problems" (Gunning 1998).

Materials

- "Word Pyramid Graphic Organizer" model" (page 115)
- "Blank Word Pyramid Graphic Organizer" (page 116, students can be provided with an activity sheet or they can copy the pyramid from the board or document camera)

Directions

1. Explain to students that often when letters are added to, or rearranged in a word, the sounds they make can change.

   Example: "mad"

   Add an "e" at the end and it becomes "made"

2. The object of this activity is to begin with a vowel in the top circle. Then add a consonant to that vowel in the second set of circles to create a word. Next, in each set of circles, another letter will be added to form a new word. The previous letters must remain in each new set of circles but the letters can be rearranged in any order to create a new word. Demonstrate with the model that follows these instructions.

3. Provide students with a copy of the "Word Pyramid Graphic Organizer" on page 116, or place it on a document camera or Whiteboard while students copy it onto their papers.

4. Work together with students to create another one or two word pyramids. Allow students to work either independently, with a partner, or in a small group to create as many word pyramids as they can in a given amount of time. To incorporate the competitive aspect, challenge students, pairs, or groups to create the most pyramids in the time allotted.

5. Have students share their word pyramids as the group discusses how the sounds in various words change as the letters are rearranged.

Word Pyramid Graphic Organizer Model

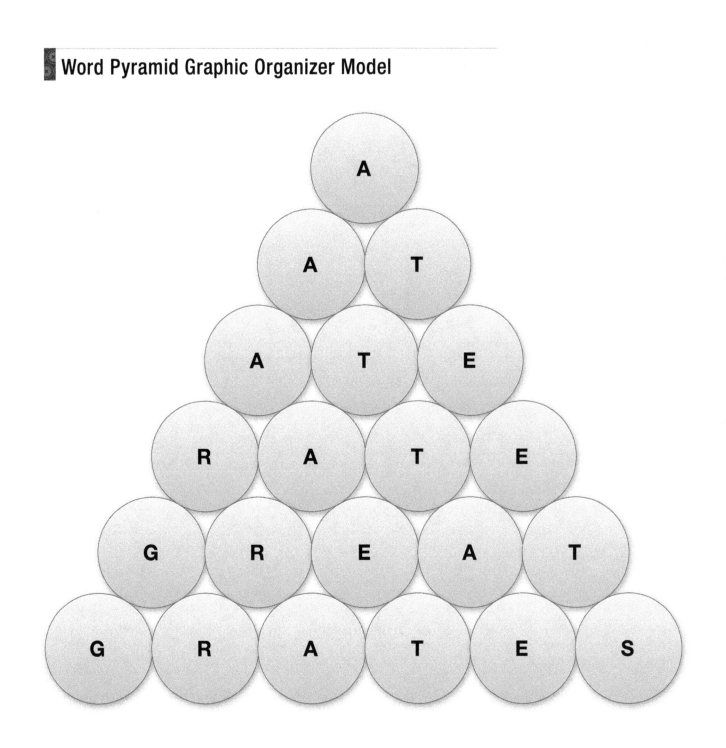

Word Pyramid Graphic Organizer

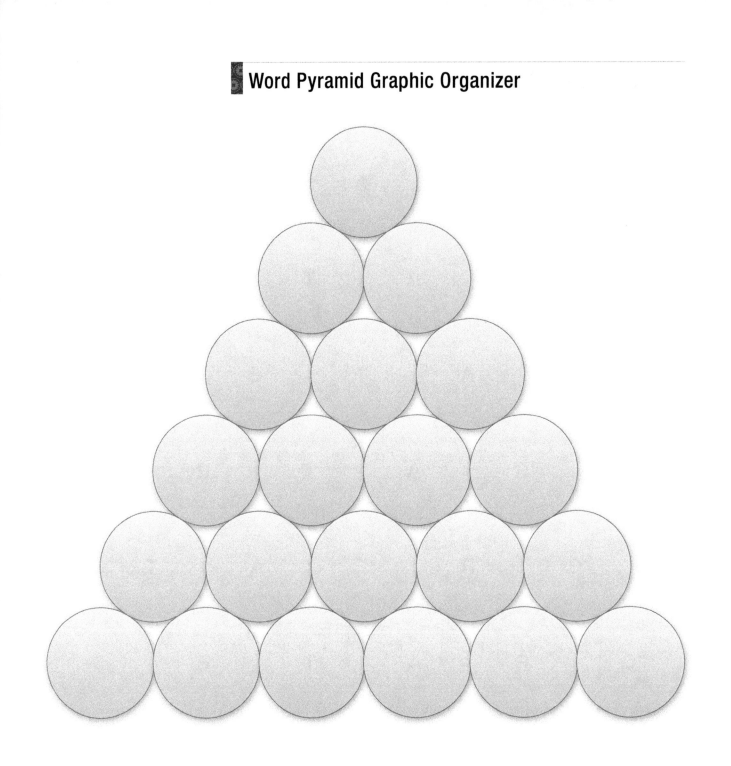

Writing Text-Dependent Questions

COMMON CORE
STATE STANDARDS
Literature 1, 2, 3, 4, 6;
Informational Text 1, 2, 3, 4, 5, 6

Objective

To recognize and write text-dependent questions and answer these questions based on textual content

What the Research Says

"Comprehension requires the reader to be an active constructor of meaning" (Wilhelm 2013).

Materials

One of the following selections: *Bronx Masquerade* by Nikki Grimes, *Twilight* by Stephenie Meyer, "Mother to Son" by Langston Hughes, or another selection for the class to read

Directions

1. Using one of the selections above, begin by sharing with students the following chart of "non-examples" and "examples" of text-dependent questions.

   ### Non-examples and Examples

   > (Questions based on *Bronx Masquerade* by Nikki Grimes, published by Dial Books for Young Readers, 2001, *Twilight* by Stephenie Meyer and published by Little, Brown and Company, 2005, and "Mother to Son" by Langston Hughes, which can be found in *Selected Poems of Langston Hughes* from Vintage Classics, 1990). For more chart examples and information on writing text-dependent questions, visit Achieve the Core on the web.

Non-text-dependent	Text-dependent
In *Bronx Masquerade*, Gloria is having difficulty being a mother and a student. Describe a time when you had difficulty managing your time.	Explain how Gloria's view on having a baby and Lupe's view on having a baby compare.
In *Twilight*, Bella is attracted to both Edward and Jacob. Describe a time when you had to make a choice.	Bella is attracted to both Edward and Jacob. Compare the characteristics, both positive and negative, of both Edward and Jacob.
In the poem "Mother to Son" by Langston Hughes, a mother is describing her hard life to her son. Describe a time in your life that was difficult.	According to Langston Hughes in his poem "Mother to Son," life is hard. Using the figurative language in the poem as a basis, literally describe the mother's life to her son.

2. Share with students the difference between the non-text-dependent example and the text-dependent example for the selection you have chosen. Discuss how the non-text-dependent example question can be answered without reading the text while the text-dependent question can only be answered by reading the text.

3. Following the gradual release model of "I do," "We do," "You do," you have just done the "I do."

4. Next, as a class, work together to have students come up with other questions that are text-dependent. You can assist them by asking them to locate important details in the selection and then work together to turn these details into questions ("We do").

5. Place students' questions on the document camera for others to view and answer as the class determines if they are actually text-dependent questions.

6. Next, provide another selection for students to read. Instruct students to write at least one text-dependent question ("You do").

7. Place students' text-dependent questions on the document camera or board for the class to answer. At this time, students are able to discuss whether the questions are actually text dependent and whether they are of high, medium, or low text complexity (see "Stems for Writing Questions at Low, Medium, and High Cognitive Levels" on pages 62 and 63).

You Are the Character!

Objective

To role play and become a character by speaking his or her words with proper expression and voice

What the Research Says

"Asking students to 'say it like the character' prompts them to make inferences about characters' feelings and voices and to bring these inferences to bear on interpretive re-readings of text, incorporate intonation inflection, and expression" (Prescott-Griffin and Witherell 2004).

Materials

- Narrative text with dialogue
- Paper
- Pencils

Directions

1. Provide students with a narrative text that contains a lot of dialogue.

2. Have students select a character that they'd like to "be."

3. Have each student select a section of text he or she would like to read where the character chosen is speaking. This should be a section of text where the character has several sentences of dialogue with at least one other character.

4. Instruct students to determine the other character or characters they will be talking to during the reading of their text chunks.

5. Students must then form groups so that they have all of the characters conversing in their chunk of text working together. Most often, students will form groups by themselves; those who don't can place the characters' names they need on the board and have other students volunteer to be a part of their conversation. Students can be in more than one group if necessary.

6. Allow time for students to work in their groups to read, re-read, and make inferences about how the character feels during this conversation. Are the characters happy, worried, scared, excited, melancholy, angry, etc.?

7. After practicing, each group writes two or three questions to ask the class after their presentation. These questions should refer to how the characters were feeling as they spoke their lines, what caused these feelings, or how the characters' dialogue moved the plot along.

8. Each group then shares their dialogue with the class as they become their characters by using proper intonation. Once each group completes their presentation, they ask the questions they wrote to the class.

9. Complete this activity with a whole-group discussion on the importance of accuracy in word decoding, automaticity in word recognition, and prosody in the reading of oral text as it relates to the meaning of the text.

ADDITIONAL RESOURCES

Alternative Assessment Ideas

COMPREHENSION

Anticipation Box

Instruct students to create a box or collage of items symbolic to a selection. Then have them share three ways one or more items were symbolic to the selection.

Using Tunes to Teach Literary Elements

Instruct students to locate lyrics to one of their favorite songs. Tell them the lyrics must contain appropriate language. Students complete one or more of the following:

- Locate the figurative language in the song:
    - Similes
    - Metaphors
    - Alliteration
    - Personification
    - Onomatopoeia
- Interpret each stanza.
- Tell the theme of the song.

Making Predictions: An Activity with Movement

Upon completion of a selection or unit of study, give each student the sentences that were used for this pre-reading activity. Instruct students to provide a summary of the selection using five of the pre-reading sentences.

Reader's Theater with a Twist: From Prose to Play

After viewing the plays and responding to the comprehension questions, instruct students to do one or more of the following activities. Students can use the prose version of the selection in their text as a reference.

- Tell the major conflict in the selection and how it was resolved.
- Provide five cause/effect statements from the selection.
- Explain how the setting was integral to the plot of the selection.
- Select one or more characters and tell how the characters changed from the beginning of the selection to the end of the selection.
- Compare the prose version of the selection to the Reader's Theater version that was presented.

Frayer Model Paper Fold

Instruct students to create the Frayer Model paper fold. They then place a character from their reading selection in the center section of the Frayer Model. In one of the four corner sections they write "what the character looks like." A second section is labeled "what the character does." The third section is labeled "how the character behaves," and the final section is labeled "make a personal connection to the character." Students complete each section using facts and details from the text.

VOCABULARY

Vocabulary Graffiti Wall

Instruct each student to create a vocabulary graffiti wall, including a section for each of their vocabulary words. Each section should include the following information:

- vocabulary word
- part of speech
- synonym
- antonym
- example
- non-example
- sentence using the word and possibly a context clue

Vocabulary at Different Cognitive Levels

This assessment allows you to differentiate instruction. Provide students with vocabulary words to be assessed. Determine at which cognitive level each student should be able to define his or her vocabulary words. On top of each student's paper, write the cognitive level at which he or she should address each word. Allow students to use their vocabulary mini-books as a resource. One suggestion for the different cognitive levels is to print the vocabulary list on different colored paper. For example, students working at the "understanding" level have their vocabulary list printed on pink paper. Students working at the "analysis" level might have their vocabulary list printed on green paper.

Writing Conversations

Tell students that their task is to write a conversation between two people, two characters from a text, or two objects (two rocks, two elements from the periodic table, two plants, two animals, etc.). They must use the words in their given vocabulary list in this conversation. The conversation must include at least three sentences with the tag (person or object talking) at the beginning, three sentences with the tag in the middle, and three sentences with the tag at the end. The vocabulary words used must be highlighted or underlined.

Examples:

Tag at the beginning: Lebron said, "What's going on tonight?"

Tag in the middle: Nothing much," said Nate, "that I know of."

Tag at the end: "Well, let's make something transpire!" said Lebron.

Linear Array

Provide students with a list of vocabulary words they are responsible for knowing, and instruct them to write a linear array for each word.

Words to Pictures

This is an excellent vocabulary review activity, especially when students have an extensive list of vocabulary words. Instruct students to locate vocabulary words to describe a character in a story selection. The students task is to draw a character likeness and place vocabulary words on the appropriate character body part. The arms and legs will contain words that describe what the character does. The heart area will contain words that describe the character's feelings. The head will contain words that describe what the character thinks, and the face will contain words that describe what the character says. Any other words that describe the character can be placed around the character. Students can then write a descriptive paragraph using the words to describe what the character does, how the character feels and thinks, and what the character says. Students are instructed to use specific examples from the story selection in their commentaries. (See *Active Word Play* by Jane Feber, Maupin House, 2008, for a character body template or locate one on the Internet.)

FLUENCY

You Are the Character!

Allow students to work with a partner or small group to select a section of text they will present to you. Students must practice their lines and be prepared to read fluently. You will listen to the students while using a fluency checklist which includes the characteristics of a fluent reader:

- Does the student speak clearly?
- Does the student read with expression?
- Does the student read with prosody?

Cloze Paragraph

After completing the cloze activity, instruct students to create a new blank cloze paragraph activity that another student will complete. Once students have created a cloze paragraph, with blank spaces for another student to complete, have students trade papers. Students then complete the cloze sheet and read it to you.

DECODING

Word Pyramid

Instruct students to create a word pyramid. Once they have completed their word pyramid, their task is to show the syllable pattern in each new word. Allow students to use their syllable patterns mini-book as a resource.

Syllable Patterns

Using current vocabulary or words from the classroom word wall, instruct students to select a given number of words to divide into syllables using the syllable patterns. Instruct students to write the syllable pattern used above each chunk of the word.

CVC/CVC	CV/CVCE	CVVC
pat/tern	di/vide	Rain

Reading Interest Survey

- Do you enjoy reading? **YES** **NO**

  If YES, what genres do you enjoy reading?

  Fantasy   Drama   Romance   Science Fiction   Adventure

- Do you play video games? **YES** **NO**

  If YES, what are your favorite games? _____

- Do you surf the Internet? **YES** **NO**

  If YES, what do you enjoy reading on the Internet? _____

- Are you a sports fan? **YES** **NO**

  If YES, what sports are you interested in? _____

- Are you into movies or real-life drama? **YES** **NO**

  If YES, what movies or drama have you seen? _____

- Are you into television? **YES** **NO**

  If YES, what shows do you watch? _____

- What do you do in your free time? *Check all that apply.*

  ☐ dance   ☐ hang with friends   ☐ skateboard

  ☐ text   ☐ talk on the phone   ☐ shop

  ☐ read   ☐ play on the computer: what do you play?

Reading Suggestions From Students By Genre

Fantasy

Abhorsen trilogy by Garth Nix

Artemis Fowl series by Eoin Colfer

Earthly Knight by Janet McNaughton

Harry Potter series by J.K. Rowling

House of Night series by P.C. Cast and Kristin Cast

Hush, Hush series by Becca Fitzpatrick

Iron Kingdoms from Privateer Press

The Hobbit by J. R. R. Tolkien

The Hollow Kingdom trilogy by Clare Dunkle

The Inheritance series by Chris Paolini

The Iron Knight by Julie Kagawa

The Land of Stories: The Wishing Spell by Chris Colfer

Tuck Everlasting by Natalie Babbitt

Wolf Mark by Joseph Bruchac

Futuristic

Everlost by Neal Shusterman

The Age of Miracles by Karen Thompson Walker

The City of Embers series by Jeanne DuPrau

The Giver by Lois Lowry

The Hunger Games series by Suzanne Collins

Uglies series by Scott Westerfeld

UnWholly by Neal Shusterman

Unwind by Neal Shusterman

Realistic Fiction

Books by Zane

Chopsticks by Jessica Anthony and Rodrigo Corral

Liar and Spy by Rebecca Stead

Period 8 by Chris Crutcher

Somewhere in the Darkness by Walter Dean Myers

Stuck in Neutral by Terry Trueman

The Help by Kathryn Stockett

Thirteen Reasons Why by Jay Asher

Mystery

Agatha Christie novels

Confessions of a Murder Suspect by James Patterson and Maxine Paetro

Killer Blonde: A Jane Austen Mystery by Laura Levine

Maximum Ride series by James Patterson

Paper Towns by John Green

Pretty Little Liars series by Sara Shepard

Stephen King books

The 39 Clues series by Rick Riordan

Theodore Boone: Kid Lawyer by John Grisham

Thirteen Reasons Why by Jay Asher

Real-Life Drama

Bluford series by Paul Langan

Bronx Masquerade by Nikki Grimes

Go Ask Alice by Anonymous

Just Listen by Sarah Dessen

Smashed by Koren Zailckas

Speak by Laurie Halse Anderson

Tears of a Tiger by Sharon Draper

The Outsiders by S. E. Hinton

The Truth About Forever by Sarah Dessen

Crank by Ellen Hopkins

Glass by Ellen Hopkins

Fallout by Ellen Hopkins

Burned by Ellen Hopkins

Supernatural

Bloodlines series by Richelle Mead

The Chronicles of Vladimir Tod series by Heather Brewer

The Infernal Devices series by Cassandra Clare

The Vampire Diaries by L.J. Smith

Twilight series by Stephenie Meyer

Vampire Academy series by Richelle Mead

Graphic Novels (Capstone Graphic Revolve Series)

20,000 Leagues Under the Sea by Jules Verne, retold by Carl Bowen

Black Beauty by Anna Sewell, retold by L. L. Owens and illustrated by Jennifer Tanner

The War of the Worlds by H.G. Wells, retold by Davis Worth Miller and Katherine McLean Brevard

The Adventures of Tom Sawyer by Mark Twain, retold by M. C. Hall and illustrated by Daniel Strickland

Journey to the Center of the Earth by Jules Verne, retold by Davis Worth Miller and Katherine McLean Brevard

The Invisible Man by H.G. Wells, retold by Terry Davis and illustrated by Dennis Calero

The Legend of Sleepy Hollow by Washington Irving, retold by Blake Hoena and illustrated by Tod Smith

DC Comic Chapter Books

Super-Villains series

The Man of Steel series

The Dark Knight series

Wonder Woman series

CROSS-REFERENCE GUIDE TO STANDARDS AND ACTIVITIES

(excerpted from CoreStandards.org)

Anchor Standards: Reading

The K-12 standards on the following pages define what students should understand and be able to do by the end of each grade. They correspond to the College and Career Readiness (CCR) anchor standards below by number. The CCR and grade-specific standards are necessary complements—the former providing broad standards, the latter providing additional specificity—that together define the skills and understandings that all students must demonstrate.

Key Ideas and Details

- **CCSS.ELA-Literacy.CCRA.R.1** Read closely to determine what the text says explicitly and to make logical inferences from it. Cite specific textual evidence when writing or speaking to support conclusions drawn from the text.

- **CCSS.ELA-Literacy.CCRA.R.2** Determine central ideas or themes of a text and analyze their development; summarize the key supporting details and ideas.

- **CCSS.ELA-Literacy.CCRA.R.3** Analyze how and why individuals, events, or ideas develop and interact over the course of a text.

Craft and Structure

- **CCSS.ELA-Literacy.CCRA.R.4** Interpret words and phrases as they are used in a text, including determining technical, connotative, and figurative meanings, and analyze how specific word choices shape meaning or tone.

- **CCSS.ELA-Literacy.CCRA.R.5** Analyze the structure of texts, including how specific sentences, paragraphs, and larger portions of the text (e.g., a section, chapter, scene, or stanza) relate to each other and the whole.

- **CCSS.ELA-Literacy.CCRA.R.6** Assess how point of view or purpose shapes the content and style of a text.

Integration of Knowledge and Ideas

- **CCSS.ELA-Literacy.CCRA.R.7** Integrate and evaluate content presented in diverse media and formats including, visually and quantitatively, as well as in words.

- **CCSS.ELA-Literacy.CCRA.R.8** Delineate and evaluate the argument and specific claims in a text, including the validity of the reasoning as well as the relevance and sufficiency of the evidence.

- **CCSS.ELA-Literacy.CCRA.R.9** Analyze how two or more texts address similar themes or topics in order to build knowledge or to compare the approaches the authors take.

Range of Reading and Level of Text Complexity

- **CCSS.ELA-Literacy.CCRA.R.10** Read and comprehend complex literary and informational texts independently and proficiently.

Anchor Standards: Speaking and Listening

The K-12 standards on the following pages define what students should understand and be able to do by the end of each grade. They correspond to the College and Career Readiness (CCR) anchor standards below by number. The CCR and grade-specific standards are necessary complements—the former providing broad standards, the latter providing additional specificity—that together define the skills and understandings that all students must demonstrate.

Comprehension and Collaboration

- **CCSS.ELA-Literacy.CCRA.SL.1** Prepare for and participate effectively in a range of conversations and collaborations with diverse partners, building on others' ideas and expressing their own clearly and persuasively.

- **CCSS.ELA-Literacy.CCRA.SL.2** Integrate and evaluate information presented in diverse media and formats, including visually, quantitatively, and orally.
  - Found Poems . . . . page 30
  - Rap It Out . . . . page 64
  - Reader's Theater with a Twist: From Prose to Play. . . . . .page 66
  - Using Cell Phones and Audacity to Become a More Fluent Reader . .page 93
  - You Are the Character! . . . . page 120

- **CCSS.ELA-Literacy.CCRA.SL.3** Evaluate a speaker's point of view, reasoning, and use of evidence and rhetoric.
  - You Are the Character! . . . . page 120

Presentation of Knowledge and Ideas

- **CCSS.ELA-Literacy.CCRA.SL.4** Present information, findings, and supporting evidence such that listeners can follow the line of reasoning and the organization, development, and style are appropriate to task, purpose, and audience.
  - Cloze Paragraph . . . . page 20
  - Found Poems . . . . page 30
  - Rap It Out . . . . page 64
  - Reader's Theater with a Twist: From Prose to Play. . . . . .page 66
  - You Are the Character! . . . . page 120

- **CCSS.ELA-Literacy.CCRA.SL.5** Make strategic use of digital media and visual displays of data to express information and enhance understanding of presentations.
  - Found Poems . . . . page 30
  - Rap It Out . . . . page 64
  - Reader's Theater with a Twist: From Prose to Play. . . . . .page 66
  - Using Cell Phones and Audacity to Become a More Fluent Reader . .page 93

- **CCSS.ELA-Literacy.CCRA.SL.6** Adapt speech to a variety of contexts and communicative tasks, demonstrating command of formal English when indicated or appropriate.
  - Cloze Paragraph . . . . page 20
  - Fluency Phrasing. . . . . page 27
  - Rap It Out . . . . page 64
  - Reader's Theater with a Twist: From Prose to Play. . . . . .page 66
  - Using Cell Phones and Audacity to Become a More Fluent Reader . .page 93
  - You Are the Character! . . . . page 120

English Language Arts Standards | Reading: Foundational Skills

- CCSS.ELA-Literacy.RF.4.3 and CCSS.ELA-Literacy.RF.5.3

Phonics and Word Recognition

- CCSS.ELA-Literacy.RF.4.3a Use combined knowledge of all letter-sound correspondences, syllabication patterns, and morphology (e.g., roots and affixes) to read accurately unfamiliar multisyllabic words in context and out of context.

LIST OF ACTIVITIES AND REPRODUCIBLES

ACTIVITY	REPRODUCIBLE
Before/During/After Reading Mini-book	GRADING RUBRIC FOR AFTER-READING ACTIVITY
Before/During/After Reading Mini-book	BEFORE, DURING, AND AFTER READING STRATEGIES MINI-BOOK
Close Paragraph	CLOZE ACTIVITY SHEET
Creating Words: Card Game	PREFIX CARDS
Creating Words: Card Game	ENDING CARDS
Fluency Phrasing	FLUENCY PHRASING ACTIVITY SHEET
Found Poems	FOUND POEM FROM *FAHRENHEIT 451* BY RAY BRADBURY
Found Poems	FOUND POEM CRITIQUE SHEET
I'm Going to…	BEGINNING/ENDING SOUNDS EXIT SLIPS
Knock-Knock Jokes Mini-book	KNOCK-KNOCK JOKE PEER REVIEW
Linear Array	SYNONYMS FOR "BIG"
Making Predictions: An Activity with Movement	EXAMPLE SENTENCE STRIPS
Object Boxes	OBJECT BOX TEMPLATE
Raising Rigor: Questions at Different Cognitive Levels	STEMS FOR WRITING QUESTIONS AT LOW, MEDIUM, AND HIGH COGNITIVE LEVELS
Reader's Theater with a Twist: From Prose to Play	READER'S THEATER COMPREHENSION QUESTION STEMS
Reader's Theater with a Twist: From Prose to Play	READER'S THEATER CRITIQUE SHEET
Reader's Theater with a Twist: From Prose to Play	READER'S THEATER GRADING RUBRIC
Reading Strategies Bookmark and Mini-book	READING STRATEGIES BOOKMARK
Syllable Patterns Mini-book	SYLLABLE PATTERNS TEACHER PAGE
Using Cell Phones and Audacity to Become a More Fluent Reader	FLUENCY PLAYBACK CRITIQUE SHEET
Viewing Movies: A Graphic Organizer for Fiction and Nonfiction	MOVIE-VIEWING GRAPHIC ORGANIZER FOR FICTION
Viewing Movies: A Graphic Organizer for Fiction and Nonfiction	VIDEO-VIEWING GRAPHIC ORGANIZER FOR NONFICTION
Vocabulary 8 Squares	VOCABULARY 8 SQUARES CRITIQUE SHEET
Vocabulary Madness	VOCABULARY MADNESS MATRIX
Vocabulary Madness	VOCABULARY MADNESS MATRIX MODEL
Vocabulary Madness	VOCABULARY MADNESS RATIONALE
Vocabulary Madness	VOCABULARY MADNESS RATIONALE MODEL
Vocabulary Mini-book: Different Cognitive Levels	VOCABULARY MINI-BOOK TEMPLATE
Word Pyramid	WORD PYRAMID GRAPHIC ORGANIZER MODEL
Word Pyramid	WORD PYRAMID GRAPHIC ORGANIZER

REFERENCES

Adams, M. J., Foorman, B. R., Lundberg, I., and Beeler, T. 1998. "The elusive phoneme: Why phonemic awareness is so important and how to help children develop it." *American Educator*, 22: 18-29.

Allen, Janet. 1999. *Words, Words, Words: Teaching Vocabulary in Grades 4-12*. Portland, ME: Stenhouse.

———. 2007. *Inside Words*. Portland, ME: Stenhouse.

Allington, Richard. 1983. "Fluency: The neglected goal." *The Reading Teacher*, 36: 556-561.

———. 2009. *What Really Matters in Fluency: Research-Based Practices across the Curriculum*. Boston, MA: Pearson.

Allyn, P. 2013. *Be Core Ready: Powerful, Effective Steps to Implementing and Achieving the Common Core State Standards*. Boston, MA: Pearson.

Armbruster, B., and Osborn, J. 2001. *Put Reading First: The Research Building Blocks for Teaching Children to Read*. Washington, D.C.: Partnership for Reading.

Beck, I., McKeown, M., and Kucan, L. 2002. *Bringing Words to Life*. New York, NY: Guilford Press.

Beers, Kylene. 2002. *When Kids Can't Read: What Teachers Can Do*. Portsmouth, NH: Heinemann.

Bhattarya, A., and Ehri, L. 2004. "Graphosyllable analysis helps adolescent struggling readers read and spell words." *Journal of Learning Disabilities*, 3: 331-348.

Bill and Melinda Gates Foundation. 2006. "The Silent Epidemic: Perspectives of High School Dropouts." *The Philanthropic New Digest: A Service of the Foundation Center*, March 3.

Blachowicz, Camille, and Fisher, Peter. 2001. *Teaching Vocabulary in All Classrooms*. 2nd ed. Boston, MA: Pearson/Prentice Hall.

———. 2004. "Keep the 'FUN' in Fundamental: Encouraging Word Awareness and Incidental Word Learning in the Classroom through Word Play." In *Vocabulary Instruction: Research to Practice*, eds. J.F. Bauman and E.J. Kame'enui. (New York: Guilford Press.)

Blackburn, B. R. 2008. *Rigor is NOT a Four-Letter Word*. New York, NY: Eye on Education.

Bradbury, R. (1953) 2012. *Fahrenheit 451*. New York: Ballantine. Reprint, New York: Simon and Schuster. Citations refer to the Simon and Schuster edition.

Bradley, L., and Bryant, P. 1983. "Categorizing sounds and learning to read: A causal connection." *Nature*, 301: 419-421.

Calkins, L. M. 2001. *The Art of Teaching Reading*. Boston, MA: Addison-Wesley Longman.

Carlisle, J.F., and Stone, C. A. (2005). "Exploring the Role of Morphemes in Word Reading." *Reading Research Quarterly*, 40(4): 428-449.

Chall, J. S. and Popp, H. M. 1997. *Teaching and Assessing Phonics: Why, What, When, How*. Cambridge, MA: Educators Publishing Service.

Cooper, J. D., Chard, D. J., and Kiger, N. D. 2006. *The Struggling Reader: Interventions That Work*. New York, NY: Scholastic, 65.

Dahl, Michael. 2010. *Knock Your Socks Off: A Book of Knock-Knock Jokes*. Mankato, MN: Picture Window Books.

Daniels, Harvey, and Steineke, Nancy 2011. *Texts and Lessons for Content-Area Reading*. Heinemann: Portsmouth, NH.

———. 2013. *Texts and Lessons for Teaching Literature*. Heinemann: Portsmouth, NH.

Dowson, M., and McInerney, D.M. 2001. "Psychological parameters of students' social and work avoidance goals: A qualitative investigation." *Journal of Educational Psychology*, 93: 35-42.

Ehri, Linnea C. 1998. "Research on learning to read and spell: A personal-historical perspective." *Scientific Studies of Reading*, 2: 97-114.

Feber, Jane. 2004. *Creative Book Reports: Fun Projects with Rubrics for Fiction and Nonfiction*. Gainesville, FL: Maupin House.

———. 2011. *Student Engagement Is FUNdamental: Building a Learning Community with Hands-on Activities*. Gainesville, FL: Maupin House.

Grady, D. 2006. *Deadly Invaders*. London, England: Kingfisher.

Grimes, Nikki. 2001. *Bronx Masquerade*. New York, NY: Dial Books for Young Readers.

Gunning, T. G. 1998. *Assessing and Correcting Reading and Writing Difficulties*. 2nd ed. Boston, MA: Allyn and Bacon.

Harvey, S., and Goudvis, A. 2007. *Strategies That Work: Teaching Comprehension to Enhance Understanding*. Portland, ME: Stenhouse.

Hughes, Langston. 1990. *Selected Poems of Langston Hughes*. New York, NY: Vintage Classics.

Jago, Carol. 2011. *With Rigor for All: Meeting Common Core Standards for Reading Literature*. Portsmouth, NH: Heinemann.

Johnson, C., and Johnson, D. 2012. *Why Teach Vocabulary?* Austin, TX: Anaxos, Inc.

Kamil, M.L. 2004. "Vocabulary and comprehension instruction: Summary and implications of the National Reading Panel findings." In *The voice of evidence in reading research*, eds. P. McCardle and V. Chhabra. (Baltimore, MD: Paul H. Brookes).

Kelley, M. J., and Clausen-Grace, N. 2007. *Comprehension Shouldn't Be Silent: From Strategy Instruction to Student Independence*. Newark, DE: International Reading Association.

Leu, D. 2002. "The New Literacies: Research on Reading Instruction with the Internet." *What Research Has to Say About Reading Instruction*, 3rd ed. International Reading Association, 2002.

Liberman, I. Y., Shankweiler, D., and Liberman, A. M. 1989. "The alphabetic principle and learning to read." In *Phonology and Reading Disability: Solving the Reading Puzzle*. Research Monograph Series, eds. Shankweiler and I. Y. Liberman. (Ann Arbor, MI: University of Michigan Press).

Marzano, Robert. 2004. *Building Background Knowledge for Academic Achievement: Research on What Works in Schools*. Alexandria, VA: ASCD.

Marzano, R., and Pickering, D. 2005. *Building Academic Vocabulary.* Alexandria, VA: ASCD.

Meyer, Stephanie. 2005. *Twilight.* New York, NY: Little Brown and Company

National Center for Research on Teacher Learning. 1993. "How Teachers Learn to Engage Students in Active Learning." Michigan State University College of Education, November. http://ncrtl.msu.edu/http/teachers.pdf.

National Governors Association Center for Best Practices and Council of Chief State School Officers. 2010. *Common Core State Standards.* Washington, D.C.: National Governors Association Center for Best Practices, Council of Chief State School Officers.

National Reading Panel. 2000. "National Reading Panel Reports Combination of Teaching Phonics, Word Sounds, Giving Feedback on Oral Reading Most Effective Way to Teach Reading," National Institute of Child Health and Human Development, April 13.

Pearson, P.D., and Gallagher, M.C. 1983. "The instruction of reading comprehension." *Contemporary Educational Psychology*, 8: 317-344.

Prescott-Griffin, M. L., and Witherell, N. L. 2004. *Fluency in Focus: Comprehension Strategies for All Young Readers.* Portsmouth, NH: Heinemann.

RAND Reading Study Group. 2002. *Reading for Understanding: Toward a Research and Development Program in Reading Comprehension.* Santa Monica, CA: Office of Education Research and Improvement.

Rasinski, Timothy. 2003. *The Fluent Reader: Oral Reading Strategies for Building Word Recognition, Fluency, and Comprehension.* New York, NY: Scholastic.

———. 2004a. *Assessing Reading Fluency.* Honolulu, HI: Pacific Resources for Education and Learning.

———. 2004b. "Creating fluent readers." *Educational Leadership*, 61(6): 46-51.

Rasinski, T., Padak, N., McKeon, C., Wilfong, L., Friedauer, J., and Heim, P. 2005. "Is Reading Fluency a Key for Successful High School Reading?" *Journal of Adolescent and Adult Literacy*, 49(1)): 22-27.

Robb, Laura. 1996. *Reading Strategies that Work*. New York, NY: Scholastic.

Routman, R. 2003. *Reading Essentials: The Specifics You Need to Teach Reading Well*. Portsmouth, NH: Heinemann.

Ryan, S., and Frazee, D. 2012. *Common Core Standards for Middle School English Language Arts*. Alexandria, VA: ASCD.

The Schelchty Center for Leadership in School Reform. 2009. "Theory of Engagement." Kent State University Science Learning Community, April 27. http://www.cs.kent.edu/~volkert/science-learning/files/Schelchty-engagement.pdf.

Shanahan, T. 2012/2013. "The Common Core Ate My Baby and Other Urban Legends." *Educational Leadership* 70 (4): 11-16.

Shanahan, T., Fisher, D., and Frey, N. 2012. "The Challenge of Challenging Text." *Educational Leadership* 69 (6): 61.

Stahl, S.A., and Kapinus, B. 2001. *Word Power: What Every Educator Needs to Know about Teaching Vocabulary*. Washington, D.C.: National Education Association.

Study Group on the Conditions of Excellence in American Higher Education. (1984, October). *Involvement in Learning: Realizing the Potential of American Higher Education*. Washington, DC: National Institute of Education.

Tovani, Chris. 2000. *I Read It, But I Don't Get It*. Portland, ME: Stenhouse.

———. 2004. *Do I Really Have to Teach Reading?* Portland, ME: Stenhouse.

Trueman, T. 2000. *Stuck in Neutral*. Des Moines, IA: Hampton-Brown.

Urquhart, V., and Frazce, D. 2012. "Challenging Texts? No Problem." *Middle Ground*, 16(2): 15.

Wilhelm, J. 2013. "Understanding Reading Comprehension." *Scholastic Teachers*, May 10. http://www.scholastic.com/teachers/article/understanding-reading-comprehension.

Zimmer, Ben. 2010. "GHOTI." *On Language: The New York Times Magazine*, June 27. http://www.nytimes.com/2010/06/27/magazine/27FOB-onlanguage-t.html?_r=0.